Mastering

Microsoft Copilot

Your Expert Guide to Enhancing Efficiency, Accuracy and Unlocking the Secrets to Seamless & Smarter Programming for Project Dominance

Blaze Hawthorn

TABLE OF CONTENTS

CHAPTER 1
INTRODUCTION TO MICROSOFT COPILOT

Microsoft Copilot is a tool for artificial intelligence (AI) that was made by Open AI and Microsoft together. Its purpose is to help developers write code by giving them ideas, auto-completion, and code snippets. Copilot uses machine learning models that have been taught on a huge amount of publicly available code to be able to generate smart code.

Developers can add Copilot to their code tools or Integrated Development Environments (IDEs) to get ideas and completions as they write code in real-time. Many programming languages and systems can be used with Copilot, which makes it a useful tool for developers in many fields. Copilot wants to boost productivity, cut down on repeated coding tasks, and give developers relevant and context-aware code ideas by looking at the context of the code being written and using its learned models. Based on the trends it has learned from the training data, it helps make code snippets, complete lines of code, and even suggest whole functions or classes. It is important to remember that Copilot can give you good ideas and code bits, but you should be careful when you use it. The code that is created should be checked by developers to make sure it meets their needs, follows best practices, and meets security standards. In general, Microsoft Copilot wants to be a strong coding assistant that uses AI to speed up the development process and help developers write code more quickly.

What is Microsoft Copilot?

Microsoft Copilot is a code completion tool driven by AI that was made by GitHub and OpenAI working together. It was made to help developers write code faster by suggesting code based on the context and notes and creating code snippets based on those features. To find useful code snippets, Copilot looks at the code environment, which includes the programming language, libraries used, and comments. It is based on OpenAI's GPT (Generative Pre-trained Transformer) design, which is the same one that is used in GPT-3 and other language models.

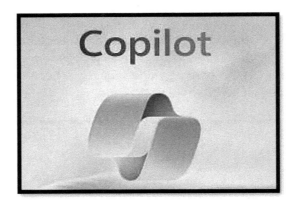

GitHub Copilot is built into several popular code editors, like Visual Studio Code, so workers can use its features right from their development environment. It can help you write functions, finish code blocks, generate documentation, and do other things. It's important to remember, though, that Copilot can be useful for developers, it's not an alternative for learning how to code or writing code that is secure and works well. Still, developers should check the suggestions that Copilot gives them to make sure they fit with the needs of the project and best practices. Also, like any AI-based tool, Copilot's suggestions might not always be right and might need to be fixed or improved manually. The way Microsoft 365 Copilot works is by combining data from a large language model (LLM) with the data that is safely stored in the documents, files, and chats in your company's Microsoft 365 tenant. Why should you use Copilot for Microsoft 365? Because it can get real-time data from the channels, events, and papers you have access to in M365. Free data is used to build the large language model, which is stored in the Microsoft Cloud by the Azure OpenAI service. But Microsoft Graph makes it safe to view your files, papers, and chats. No one else can see this data, and it's not used to teach the AI anything.

History and Development

Microsoft Copilot was made by GitHub, which is a Microsoft Company, and OpenAI working together. It was made possible by improvements in AI technology, especially OpenAI's GPT (Generative Pre-trained Transformer) design, which runs language models like GPT-3.

In brief, here is a background of Microsoft Copilot and how it has changed over time:

1. **GitHub Acquisition by Microsoft (2018):** In June 2018, Microsoft bought GitHub, which is the biggest site for storing and working together on code repositories. This purchase showed that Microsoft wanted to help open-source groups and developers.

2. **Integration of AI Technologies:** After being bought, GitHub started looking into ways to improve the developer experience by adding AI technologies to its platform. This led to working together with OpenAI, a group that does study on artificial intelligence.
3. **Emergence of OpenAI's GPT Models:** OpenAI created several versions of its GPT (Generative Pre-trained Transformer) models, which showed amazing skills in understanding and creating normal language. These models were taught on huge amounts of text data from the internet, which lets them write text that sounds like it was written by a person when they are told to.
4. **Development of Copilot Concept:** GitHub and OpenAI worked together to look into making a code completion tool based on GPT technology because they saw how AI could help developers. The goal of this tool was to help developers write code more quickly and correctly by giving them contextual code ideas.
5. **Testing and Iteration:** A lot of testing and iteration went into making Copilot so that the AI model could do more and work better with more programming languages, tools, and frameworks. GitHub probably talked to a group of workers to get opinions and ideas during this process.
6. **Announcement and Public Release:** Microsoft Copilot was first talked about at GitHub's Universe event in June 2021. At first, it was only offered to a small group of people as a technical preview. Over time, Copilot was improved based on comments from users, and in the end, it was made available to all GitHub users.
7. **Integration with Visual Studio Code:** As part of Microsoft's larger plan to add AI features to developer tools, Copilot was added to Visual Studio Code, which is one of the most famous code editors used by developers around the world. With this integration, developers could use Copilot's features right from their working platform.
8. **Continued Development and Improvement:** Microsoft Copilot is still being developed and improved after it was released to the public. GitHub and OpenAI may be working on making the AI model even more accurate, adding more languages it can understand, and fixing any problems or restrictions users have found.

Overall, the creation of Microsoft Copilot is a big step forward in the area where AI and software development meet. The goal is to give workers more power and make the coding process easier by intelligently completing and helping with code.

Key Features

Microsoft Copilot has a few important tools that make coding easier for developers:

1. **AI-Powered Code Suggestions:** Copilot uses powerful machine learning algorithms built on OpenAI's GPT (Generative Pre-trained Transformer) architecture to look at the context of the code and make suggestions that make sense. It knows many programming languages, tools, and frameworks, which lets it give accurate suggestions that make sense in the given situation.

2. **Contextual Code Completion:** Copilot gives smart suggestions for how to finish writing code based on what is being written at the moment. It can make whole functions, whole blocks of code, and suggestions for variable names, which saves developers time and work.
3. **Code Snippet Generation:** Copilot can do more than just finish off pieces of code; it can also make whole chunks of code based on notes or natural language descriptions given by the coder. This feature is especially helpful for quickly making prototypes of solutions or putting complicated methods into action.
4. **Language Support:** Microsoft Copilot works with a lot of popular computer languages, such as JavaScript, Python, Java, C++, and many more. Because it supports so many languages, people from a wide range of fields and platforms can use it.
5. **Integration with Visual Studio Code:** One of the most famous code editors used by developers, Visual Studio Code, works well with Copilot. This integration lets workers use Copilot's features right from their development platform, which makes them more productive and improves the efficiency of their work.
6. **Code Quality and Best Practices:** Copilot's suggestions are based on best coding practices and standard ways of writing code. It can help improve the quality of code by making sure it is consistent, finding possible mistakes or bugs, and offering fixes or changes that are better.
7. **Learning and Collaboration:** The AI model keeps learning and getting better over time as developers use Copilot and its suggestions in their code. These steps encourage developers and the AI to work together, where both can gain from the other's ideas and knowledge.
8. **Accessibility:** Copilot is great for workers of all levels, from those who are just starting to learn how to code to those who are working on very complicated projects. It gives developers helpful tips and advice throughout the coding process, so they can focus on fixing problems and coming up with new solutions.
9. **Security and Privacy:** Microsoft Copilot puts security and privacy first by taking steps to keep private data and code safe. It follows the privacy settings and rights that users have set and makes sure that the code snippets that Copilot creates don't reveal private data or break security rules.

Microsoft Copilot is a productivity tool that uses AI to connect your data across Microsoft Graph and Microsoft 365 services and apps, such as Word, Outlook, Excel, PowerPoint, Teams, and more. Microsoft Copilot uses natural language processing and machine learning techniques to figure out what's going on and make smart suggestions. This means that Copilot has learned from a huge amount of data, which includes code.

These are some of the most important things about Microsoft Copilot for Microsoft 365:

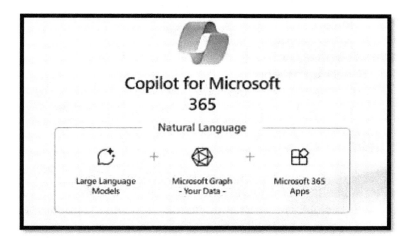

- **Large language models (LLMs)**: Copilot uses LLMs to understand how users behave, look at data, make specific suggestions, give advice, and do things automatically.
- **Integration with Microsoft Graph**: Copilot connects to Microsoft Graph so you can get to your data in Microsoft 365 apps and services.
- **Natural language processing (NLP)**: Natural language processing, or NLP, helps Copilot figure out what the user is trying to say and give them the right answer.
- **Task automation**: Copilot can do things like making reports, arranging meetings, and writing code snippets automatically.
- **Real-time collaboration**: Copilot can help teams work together by giving them ideas and tips in real time.

Overall, these key features make Microsoft Copilot a useful tool for developers that help them write code faster, make it better, and work together on software projects more effectively.

Microsoft 365 Copilot Features

There are two ways that Copilot works with Microsoft 365. It works with the user and is built into the Microsoft 365 apps you use every day, like Word, Excel, PowerPoint, Outlook, Teams, etc., to make you more productive, give you better access to data, and generally teach you more.

Here are some of the tools that are known to be part of the Microsoft 365 package with Copilot.

Copilot features in Word

With Copilot, Word now has the best tool for writing, editing, accessing, adding information, and summarizing as quickly and correctly as possible.

Making a first draft, adding relevant documents, including information that interests you, and giving each task a personalized tone by knowing who will be reading the document.

- Use other text papers to make summaries.
- Suggest styles of writing, such as professional and informal...
- Give reasons to back up a theory.
- Rewrite parts of the text or point out errors.
- Use outlines or frameworks to make drafts of your writing.

Copilot Features in PowerPoint

Copilot in PowerPoint can help you make great presentations out of your thoughts. If you're not very creative, Copilot will help you tell stories in the best way possible. It can turn written papers into full presentations, complete with fonts and notes to make your show stronger. Or, start a new slideshow from scratch with just an idea or topic. You can shorten long talks with the click of a button and use your natural language to change the style, reformat text, or make sure that animations run in perfect sync.

- Use information from another file to make a rough slideshow.
- Summarize presentations.
- Change how a certain slide is laid out.
- Cut down on writing and time it to match animations that are already in a slideshow.

Copilot features in Excel

Copilot in Excel is here to make it easier to look at and analyze data. Don't worry about formulas; just ask about the information you're given to get real results, correlations, and "what-if" scenarios. It will also use models to help you look into your data and offer new ways to answer your questions.

To get more information, look for trends, create visualizations, and ask for advice.

- Get rid of the highest or lowest numbers in an **Excel spreadsheet** that is full of data and factors. One good use for this is to see, for example, which groups sell the most items, where the most expensive items are, or which companies sell the most.
- Write up rough bills or books.
- Generate graphs.
- Change one of the factors to assume sales and growth.

Copilot features in Outlook

Managing our emails takes time which keeps us from being as productive as we could be. We can talk to each other better and faster with Copilot in Outlook. By summarizing long and confusing email threads with many people, you can quickly see what was said, as well as what each person thought and what questions were still unanswered. With a simple prompt, you can reply to an email or turn short notes into clear, defined messages from other Microsoft 365 emails or content you already look at.

- Use information from other papers to write drafts of emails.
- Outline message chains.
- By achieving the above two points, 'clean up' the inbox faster than usual.
- Mark the most important word or item.

Copilot features in Teams

Copilot in Microsoft Teams helps you run more productive meetings, record meeting highlights, and sum up important steps so that everyone on your team knows what to do next. Copilot answers specific questions or lets you know about anything you missed in chat. When you add Copilot to your conversations and meetings, you get a powerful tool that can help you with daily tasks like making meeting agendas based on chat history, finding the right people to follow up with, and setting up monitoring meetings.

- Make a list of things that you could talk about in meetings.
- Also, make a meeting format based on the chat notes.
- Write up meeting recaps for people who missed it, were late, or just want a summary.

Copilot features in Power Apps

With Copilot, app makers will be able to work with both machines and people to make apps faster and easier. Using natural language models, developers will make apps by having users talk about what they need. Copilot will also let users connect with data as they would with a chatbot, making it easier to ask questions and improve analysis. Power Apps now also has robots called Power Virtual Agents built in. For developers, this will make it easy to add AI chatbots to their apps. Microsoft wants to be at the forefront of low-code application creation by adding these tools. They also want to make transformative software in a language that everyone can understand.

Copilot Features in Power Automate

Copilot and Create text with GPT are two new tools that have been added to Microsoft Power Automate to make it better. When it first came out in October 2022, The Describe it to design it let you type a simple line and make a process based on that. With Copilot, the user can improve and change flows by having talks that are run by AI. Natural language is used to make simple flows or complicated business processes. Users ask questions and get help to make changes and improvements. Microsoft has also added a new feature called Create text with GPT that lets users automatically create content in PC processes. This can save time compared to manual crawling, which can be useful for customer service, making daily content, and getting information from a lot of text and papers. This means that these new features make Power Automate smarter, faster, and more effective at automating tasks.

Who Can Use Microsoft Copilot?

Microsoft Copilot is an all-in-one system that works for a wide range of users, from individuals and workers to big businesses.

Let's get into the specifics:

- **For Individuals:** Copilot is fun for individuals because it combines basic features into a single experience that works on all of your devices. It learns your habits on the web, your PC, your apps, and soon your phone to give you the right skills when you need them. It's also connected to the internet, so it always has the most up-to-date information. You get free business data protection when you sign in to Copilot with your Microsoft Entra ID. This means that chat data isn't saved, Microsoft can't see it, and it's not used to train the models.
- **For Businesses:** Business users can pick either Microsoft Copilot or Copilot for Microsoft 365. As was already said, Copilot has many business benefits that make it a great choice for companies of all kinds. Copilot is a useful tool for improving productivity and teamwork in businesses of all sizes, from small start-ups to big corporations, because it works well with other Microsoft products. Businesses can make Copilot fit their needs while keeping data safe and following the rules thanks to features and user rights that can be changed.

For Developers: Copilot's AI-powered features give developers a huge range of creative and innovative options. The features of Copilot can be used by developers to handle code jobs, make images, and help with debugging. Because it works with GitHub, Microsoft Copilot also gives you useful information for code reviews and tips for making the quality of your code better.

What Are Microsoft's Different Copilots?

Microsoft Copilot is a group of AI-powered assistants that are meant to make different parts of your life more productive and efficient. The image below sorts the different Copilots into groups based on what they can do.

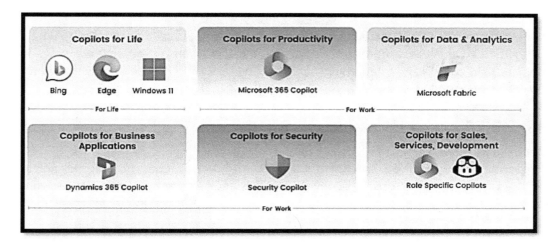

- **Copilots for Life:** You can get Microsoft Copilot (formerly Bing Chat or Bing Chat Enterprise) for free. It's great for everyday jobs and makes searching and browsing the web better, so you can find what you need faster and easier. This works great for work and play, and it's fully compatible with Windows 11 and Edge.
- **Copilot for Productivity:** Copilot for Microsoft 365 streamlines your processes and helps you get more done in less time by making smart ideas and automating tasks in Microsoft 365 apps like Word, Outlook, and Excel.
- **Data and Analytics Copilots:** These Copilots help you better handle and study your data and can be found in Microsoft Fabric. They give you useful information, help you make choices based on facts, and make your business run more smoothly.
- **Business Applications Copilot:** This Copilot is designed for business applications and works with Dynamics 365 to make your business processes and contacts with customers better. It makes smart ideas and takes care of boring jobs automatically so you can concentrate on what's important.
- **Security Copilot:** Microsoft cares a lot about your safety. The Security Copilot has cutting-edge security features that help keep private data safe and in line with regulations.
- **Sales, Services, and Development Copilots:** These are designed to help with specific business areas. Microsoft has a Copilot for everyone, whether you're a sales rep who

wants to make more sales, a service provider who wants to improve your service delivery or a developer who wants to make your coding tasks easier.

The Microsoft Copilot line includes these and other products that are meant to help you be more productive and efficient. They have many useful features and benefits that make them great for both businesses and people. Let's take a look at each Copilot individually, seeing what makes it special and how it can improve your digital life.

How to Use Microsoft Copilots for Your Everyday Life

Copilot can be your assistant and is ready to help you with projects and daily tasks on Bing, Edge, and Windows. AI makes us more productive, creative, and able to understand things better. Copilot can help you discover new things whether you're surfing the web, looking for answers, letting your creativity flow, or making useful content.

Bing: Unleash the Power of AI in Your Searches

Bing's Copilot is more than just a search engine. It turns into your personal AI assistant for all your online looking needs when you use Copilot. Copilot can answer your questions quickly and briefly, which saves you time and effort. It also gives you ideas and helps with your writing assignments, which makes it useful for both students and workers.

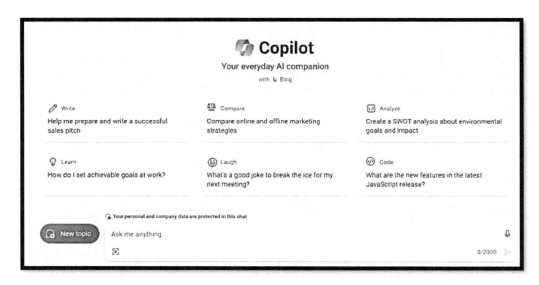

Follow these simple steps to get the most out of Bing's Copilot feature. To use Copilot in the search bar, go to Bing's home page, sign in with your Microsoft account (or make a free account), and then click "Search." Type in your question, press "Enter," and you'll get short solutions to your questions.

Edge: Your Browser Supercharged with AI

Edge is Microsoft's powerful and new web browser, and Copilot makes it even better. Edge has AI features that can help you find things faster, make viewing better, and keep your online data safe. It also works perfectly with Bing to give you a complete and quick search experience.

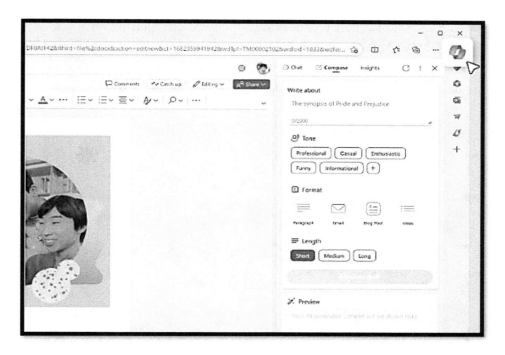

Follow these easy steps to learn how to turn on Copilot in Edge.

- Start up your Microsoft Edge browser. It can be downloaded from the Microsoft website if you don't already have it.
- Make sure your Microsoft Account is signed in. If not, use the three-dot button in the upper right corner to get to Settings and Profiles. Then, click on Add Profile to sign in or make an account.
- In the top right corner of the browser window, click on the three dots to bring up the menu. This will take you to Edge Settings.
- Go to the Settings menu and click on Privacy, search, and services.
- In the Services list, scroll down and click on Microsoft Copilot.
- To use Copilot, flip the switch to "On."

Copilot will make your Edge viewing better by giving you smart ideas and faster search results. Remember that you need to have the most recent version of Edge installed for Copilot to work properly. Regular changes add new features and make sure that your online experience is as safe as possible.

Copilot for Windows11: AI on Your Desktop

Start a change in efficiency with Copilot for Windows 11, the cutting-edge AI-powered assistant that will make your digital life better. Copilot is your smart assistant. It fits right into your work and can be found on the taskbar or by pressing Win+C on your computer. You'll be more productive because Copilot makes it easy to find answers and ideas on the web, which encourages creativity and teamwork. Its simple support will help you think less and finish your work faster. Copilot makes complicated jobs easy by streamlining processes, which makes your daily life run more smoothly.

Copilot is with you on all screen sizes, whether you're at work, school, or home, helping you with your apps. It helps you concentrate and gets things done faster when it's around.

The Role of AI in Modern Workspaces

"AI is not just a technology; it's an opportunity for humanity to redefine what's possible." AI has become a powerful force that is changing lots of different businesses and the way we work. There's no denying that it has changed settings, turning the typical office into a clever and changing ecosystem.

Enhanced Productivity and Efficiency

AI technologies can make offices more productive and easier to use. Smart automation tools can do boring and routine tasks, freeing up people to work on more important and creative projects. AI helps businesses be more efficient and productive by giving them tools like chatbots that help customers right away and data platforms that make business processes run more smoothly.

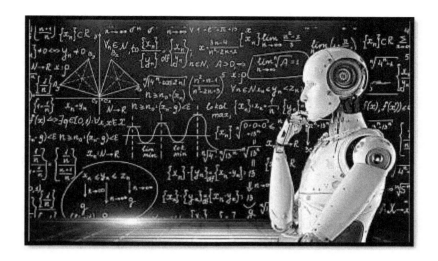

Intelligent Decision-Making

Organizations can make better choices based on data when AI is used to analyze it. Advanced algorithms can quickly sort through huge amounts of data, find trends, and come up with useful insights. From predicting market trends to improving supply chain management, AI gives business leaders the tools they need to make better decisions with more trust and accuracy.

Personalized Experiences

Systems that are driven by AI can make experiences more personalized for both workers and customers. In offices, AI can learn what each person likes, change based on their actions, and make the area fit their needs. AI makes things like personalized learning and training programs and flexible work environments more interesting and rewarding for workers. This makes them more productive and happier.

Augmented Collaboration

AI technologies make it easy for people from different teams and departments to work together and talk to each other. Intelligent virtual assistants and robots make it easier to share information in real-time and make work easier. AI-powered collaboration tools make it easy for teams in different places to work together, removing geographical hurdles and creating a more welcoming workplace.

Job Transformations and Skill Development

Adding AI to workspaces will always change the jobs that people do. Even though some boring tasks might be taken over by machines, new jobs and chances open up. Companies will need workers with new skills, such as knowing how to use AI, thinking critically, and being creative. Programs for upskilling and reskilling employees are needed to give them the skills they need to do well in an AI-driven workplace.

Today, AI plays many roles in the workplace, and these roles are changing quickly. Here are a few important ways that AI is changing and improving modern workplaces:

1. **Automation of Repetitive Tasks:** AI technologies like robotic process automation (RPA) and machine learning are being used more and more in many fields to handle tasks that are done over and over again. This includes things like data entry, handling documents, answering customer service calls, and more. By automating these routine tasks, workers can focus on more important and creative parts of their jobs.

2. **Enhanced Decision-Making:** Analytics and decision support tools that are powered by AI help organizations make better choices based on data. These systems can look at a lot of data, find patterns and trends, and give you information that helps you make smart decisions. AI-driven analytics are very important for better business results because they help with everything from personalized marketing strategies to streamlining the supply chain.

3. **Natural Language Processing (NLP) for Communication:** Virtual assistants, chatbots, and language translation tools that make it easier for people inside and outside of businesses to talk to each other are powered by NLP technologies that are driven by AI. Virtual assistants, such as chatbots, can answer simple questions, set up meetings, and give workers information. This makes contact easier and boosts productivity.

4. **Personalized Experiences:** AI makes it possible for both workers and buyers to have unique experiences. In HR, for instance, AI can look at data about employees to make sure that learning and development programs are tailored to each person's needs. In the same way, AI-powered suggestion engines can help customers find the right products based on their past purchases and habits.

5. **Improved Customer Service:** Chatbots and virtual assistants powered by AI are changing the way customer service is done by offering support 24 hours a day, seven days a week, answering common questions, and fixing problems right away. These AI systems are good at answering a lot of questions quickly, which frees up human agents to do more difficult and useful jobs.

6. **Predictive Maintenance:** In industry and other fields, AI-powered predictive maintenance systems look at data from sensors to guess when equipment will break down before it does. Companies can cut down on downtime, maintenance costs, and business inefficiency by finding possible problems early on.

7. **Augmented Creativity:** AI tools are being used more and more to help people be more creative in areas like writing, designing, and making music. AI-powered tools can help developers by, for example, coming up with ideas, making content plans, or even writing text for them. Similarly, AI can help artists by coming up with different designs based on the criteria they give it.

8. **Remote Work Enablement:** As more people choose to work from home, AI technologies are essential for making it easier for people to work together, talk to each other, and get things done in virtual spaces. Collaboration tools, virtual meeting assistants, and project management platforms that are driven by AI help teams that work remotely stay in touch and organized.

9. **Ethical and Bias Mitigation:** As AI technologies become more common in the workplace, more attention is being paid to making sure they are used honestly and ethically. More and more companies are putting money into AI ethics models, tools that find bias, and diversity programs to make sure that AI algorithms and decision-making processes aren't biased.

Overall, AI is changing modern workspaces by automating tasks, making it easier to make decisions, improving communication, making situations more personal, letting people work from home, and making people more creative. As AI gets better, it will likely have a bigger effect on the workplace, making it more efficient, creative, and competitive. But it's important to deal with problems like ethics, bias, and privacy to make sure that AI tools are used in the workplace responsibly and ethically.

Impact of Microsoft Copilot on Daily Workflows

Microsoft Copilot could have a big impact on workers' daily work by making it easier to code, making them more productive, and making it easier for people to work together.

Here are some ways that Copilot can change the way people do their daily work:

1. **Efficient Code Completion:** Copilot makes smart code completion suggestions based on what the user is writing at the moment. This can save developers time by typing parts of code that are used over and over, like import statements, function descriptions, and variable declarations.
2. **Faster Prototyping:** Copilot can create whole pieces of code based on what the coder says or writes in natural language. In this feature, solutions can be quickly prototyped, which lets developers test ideas and make changes to them without having to write all new code.
3. **Learning and Knowledge Sharing:** Copilot's ideas are built on a huge body of code from many places, such as open-source libraries. The more developers use Copilot and follow its advice, the more they can learn about new coding methods, tools, and best practices. This encourages development teams to keep learning and share what they know.
4. **Code Quality Improvement:** Copilot's ideas are based on best practices and standard ways of writing code. Copilot can help improve code quality, consistency, and maintainability across projects by making ideas that follow coding standards.
5. **Reduced Cognitive Load:** Copilot can help developers find their way around complicated codebases by giving them context-based ideas and code examples. This lowers the mental load that comes with knowing code you don't know and speeds up the process of fixing problems or making changes.
6. **Collaboration Enhancement:** Copilot can help team members work together by giving them consistent code advice and tips. Developers can use Copilot's ideas to make their coding styles and methods more consistent, which will make code reviews and merging go more smoothly.
7. **Accessibility and Inclusivity:** Copilot can help developers of all levels, even those who are just starting to learn how to code. By offering helpful direction and help throughout the

writing process, Copilot can enable people from a wide range of backgrounds and experiences to contribute more effectively to software development tasks.

8. **Integration with Development Environments:** Copilot works perfectly with popular code editors like Visual Studio Code, so workers can use its features right from the programming environment they prefer. With this integration, Copilot fits right into workers' current processes, so they don't have to switch between tools.

Overall, Microsoft Copilot could change the way developers work every day by eliminating boring tasks, letting them make quick prototypes, improving code quality, encouraging teamwork, and giving people of all skill levels more power. Since workers are already using Copilot in their daily work, its effect on productivity and new ideas in software development is likely to get stronger over time.

Use Cases That Make a Real Difference

These are some real-life things that Microsoft Copilot can do for you and your business. What's important is not so much the features and duties as the value they can bring.

1. **Kickstart Creativity**: Stop looking at Word pages that are blank. Copilot gives you a rough draft, so you can focus on making your ideas better. It gets easier and more natural to use PowerPoint presentations and Excel studies. You may have heard of ChatGPT. This is a creative AI that helps you shape your ideas into a great place to start any project you're working on.

2. **Boost Productivity:** Get ready to take on your annoying inbox and make the most of every meeting. Copilot helps you highlight meeting action points in real-time, summarize long email threads, and give you ideas for how to reply. It's amazing how quickly those little jobs that take five minutes here and there add up. That's no longer necessary with Copilot.

3. **Low Code:** Have you ever felt like Microsoft 365 apps have too many features for you to handle? We're not brave enough to deal with Access, let's face it. With Copilot, users will be able to use platforms they find hard to understand thanks to natural language orders. This will make them easier to use and give them more chances to make their jobs more useful.

4. **Always Learning:** Copilot isn't set and forget. Like any good learning model, it's made to change and adapt to new jobs and ways of doing things and to help you with whatever you're doing in general. This means it should live up to its name over time.

5. **Responsible AI:** It's clear that Microsoft is committed to responsibly developing AI. The company follows a strict AI standard that protects data privacy, limits harmful material, and makes sure everyone is treated equally. This makes sure that the AI system's decisions are clear and supports user freedom and control. A lot has been said about how algorithms can make it hard to use social media sites, so it's great to see Microsoft taking the next step in computers so seriously.

Supported Programming Languages

It works with many programming languages, like Python, JavaScript, TypeScript, C++, and more. It can be used by a lot of different developers because of this.

Differences between Copilot AI and other Virtual Assistants

Other virtual assistants, like Siri, Alexa, and Google Assistant, are very different from Microsoft Copilot AI in terms of what they can do and who they are meant for.

These are some important differences:

1. **Target Audience:**
   - **Microsoft Copilot AI:** Microsoft Copilot is mainly made for developers and is intended to help them write code faster. It gives you ideas for how to finish writing code, creates code snippets, and helps you understand what you're writing while you're writing it.
   - **Other Virtual Assistants:** Virtual assistants like Siri, Alexa, Google Assistant, and others like them are made for regular people and can do a lot of things, like play music, set notes, handle smart home devices, give you weather updates, and answer general questions.
2. **Scope of Assistance:**
   - **Microsoft Copilot AI**: Copilot's main job is to help developers with coding tasks. It suggests ways to finish off pieces of code, creates code snippets from natural language descriptions, and gives relevant help based on the code that is being written.
   - **Other Virtual Assistants:** General-purpose virtual assistants like Siri, Alexa, and Google Assistant can help with a wider range of tasks, such as managing personal tasks, getting information from the internet, controlling smart home devices, sending messages, making calls, setting reminders, and showing you how to navigate.

3. **Contextual Understanding:**
   - **Microsoft Copilot AI:** Copilot has learned to understand programming languages, tools, and coding standards by studying a huge amount of code from many different sources. It uses this information to give the developer code ideas and help that are useful to their needs.
   - **Other Virtual Assistants:** General-purpose virtual assistants can understand orders and questions written in normal language, but they don't understand the context as well as Copilot does. They do things by following pre-set orders and responses, and they might not be as good at certain things, like software creation.
4. **Integration with Development Tools:**
   - **Microsoft Copilot:** Microsoft Copilot is built into famous code editors like Visual Studio Code, so developers can use its features right from their working environment. This

tight connection makes things easier for developers and makes sure that workflows work well together.
- **Other Virtual Assistants:** You can usually get to general-purpose virtual assistants through their apps or devices, like smartphones and smart speakers, and they might not be directly built into development environments or tools.

5. **Learning and Improvement:**
   - **Microsoft Copilot AI:** Copilot keeps learning and getting better over time thanks to developer comments and the code it works with. As developers use Copilot and give feedback, the AI model changes and gets better at making ideas that are useful and correct.
   - **Other Virtual Assistants:** General-purpose virtual assistants also learn and get better over time, but they learn more about what users want, how to better understand language, and how to give better answers to general questions and tasks.

To sum up, Copilot AI and other virtual assistants use AI technologies, but they are used for different things, are aimed at different groups of people, and have unique features that are specific to their fields. Copilot is designed to help developers write code faster and more efficiently. Other virtual assistants are more general-use and offer a wider range of features for personal and home tasks.

CHAPTER 2
GETTING STARTED

It's pretty easy to get started with Microsoft Copilot, especially if you already know how to code and use code editors like Visual Studio Code.

If you want to learn how to use Microsoft Copilot, here are the steps:

1. **Install Visual Studio Code (VS Code):** If you haven't already, get Visual Studio Code and install it. It's one of the code editors that Copilot can work with.
2. **Install the GitHub Copilot Extension:** Once Visual Studio Code is set up, you need to get the GitHub Copilot extension. Open Visual Studio Code and click on the square button in the sidebar or press Ctrl+Shift+X (Windows/Linux) or Cmd+Shift+X (Mac) to go to the Extensions view. Find "GitHub Copilot" in the Extensions Marketplace and click "Install" to add the add-on.
3. **Sign in to GitHub:** You'll need to use your GitHub account to sign in to Microsoft Copilot. You will need to make a GitHub account if you don't already have one. Sign in to Visual Studio Code with your GitHub account after making an account or logging in if you already have one.
4. **Set Up GitHub Copilot:** You will need to set up GitHub Copilot after downloading the app and having logged in. To finish setting up, just follow the on-screen instructions. Usually, this means giving them access to your GitHub account and setting up any other settings that are needed.
5. **Start Coding with Copilot:** Once you've loaded and set up GitHub Copilot, you can start using it to help you write code. In Visual Studio Code, open a code file, either a new one or an old one, and start typing code. Copilot will give you code ideas and completions as you type based on what you're typing.

Setting up Microsoft Copilot

Setting up Microsoft Copilot can be fun and useful as well! Now let's begin. To help you through the process, here are some steps:

1. **Installation**:
   - First, make sure that your computer has a code editor that is compatible with it. Visual Studio Code (VS Code) is officially supported by Microsoft Copilot.
   - Open VS Code and press Ctrl+Shift+X to go to the Extensions Marketplace.
   - Look for "Copilot" and install the "GitHub Copilot" app.
   - Do what it says to do to log in with your GitHub account.
2. **Authentication**:
   - After installing the app, you'll need to sign in with your GitHub credentials.

- Click on the GitHub Copilot button in the sidebar of VS Code, then follow the on-screen prompts to sign in.
3. **Configuration**:
   - Click on the gear button in the GitHub Copilot panel to change how Copilot works for you.
   - Change settings like language support, key bindings, and how snippets work.
4. **Usage**:
   - Open an old code project or start a new one.
   - As you write code, Copilot will give you ideas, autocomplete words, and even make up whole functions based on what you're writing.
   - Press Tab or Enter to agree with Copilot's ideas.
5. **Learning and Feedback**:
   - Copilot changes as you use it and learn from the way you code.
   - If you have any problems or suggestions, you could report them through the app or the GitHub source.

Keep in mind that Copilot is a powerful tool, but it's important to understand the code it creates and fix anything wrong.

System Requirements and Installation

Microsoft recently made Copilot, its conversational AI assistant, available to more Windows 10 users. The plan seems to be to let users who are still on Windows 10 or who have devices that aren't compatible with Windows 11 try out the AI assistant. It's worth noting that 69 percent of Windows-based PC users at the time of writing are in this group. Accessing the program and being a part of it is only the beginning. People who want to use Copilot will also need to make sure their computers meet certain standards. You need at least 4GB of RAM and a display adapter that can handle at least 720p quality to do this. The preview is only available in a few areas, such as North America, some parts of Asia, and some parts of South America. No plans have been made to make it available to more people yet. Other small limits for Copilot on Windows 10 right now include not working with taskbars on the left or right side of the screen, not supporting setups with multiple monitors, and not letting Pro machines controlled by groups access. The tool is an icon on the right side of the taskbar for Windows 10 users who can get to it. It can be used to answer questions or come up with new ideas, control Windows features, work with documents, and more. When Copilot is ready, users can turn it on by clicking the button on the right side of the window. Users can ask questions, control Windows tools, and work with documents using Copilot. It works a little differently on Windows 10 because it doesn't have some Windows 11 features, but it still has a lot of AI-based features. Microsoft Copilot was a plugin available for Visual Studio Code, which is a well-known code editor. Here are the general system prerequisites and steps for setting it up:

System Requirements

1. **Operating System**:
   - Windows 10 or 11 (64-bit)
   - macOS 10.13+
   - Linux
2. **Visual Studio Code**:
   - Version 1.61.0 or later.
3. **Internet Connection**:
   - You need a stable internet connection because Microsoft Copilot uses cloud-based models.

4. **Subscription Plans**:
   - **To buy Microsoft Copilot for Microsoft 365, you need to have one of the following subscription plans:**
     - Microsoft 365 E5
     - Microsoft 365 E3
     - Office 365 E3
     - Office 365 E5
     - Microsoft 365 Business Standard
     - Microsoft 365 Business Premium
     - Microsoft 365 A5 for faculty*
     - Microsoft 365 A3 for faculty*
     - Office 365 A5 for faculty*
     - Office 365 A3 for faculty*

Note: People who have an Education or Business plan that doesn't include Teams can still buy Copilot licenses.

5. **Base Licenses**:
   - For your users to get a Copilot for Microsoft 365 license, they must already have one of the base licenses listed above.
   - Plans like Microsoft 365 E5, E3, Office 365 E3, E5, and others that meet the requirements are needed.
6. **Microsoft 365 Apps**:
   - Desktop apps from Microsoft 365, like Word, Excel, PowerPoint, Outlook, and Teams, need to be set up.
   - Once a license is given, Copilot will also be available in the web versions of the apps.
7. **OneDrive Account**:
   - To use some parts of Copilot for Microsoft 365, like restoring files and managing OneDrive, users need to have an OneDrive account.
8. **Outlook for Windows**:
   - Use the new Outlook (Windows, Mac, Web, and Mobile) for smooth integration. Classic Outlook (Windows) can also be used with Copilot.

9. **Microsoft Teams**:
   - Use the Teams PC client or web client to use Copilot in Microsoft Teams. It works with both the old and new versions of Teams.

Before you install, you should make sure of the following:

1. **Purchase Licenses**: The Microsoft 365 admin center, Microsoft partners, or the Microsoft account team are all places where you can buy Copilot for Microsoft 365 licenses.
2. **Assign Licenses**: Give Copilot licenses to people who are qualified based on the base licenses they already have.
3. **Configure OneDrive**: Make sure users have OneDrive accounts so that Copilot can do everything it can.
4. **Set up Outlook**: For the best Copilot interaction, use the new Outlook. You can also use the old version of Outlook.
5. **Enable Copilot in Teams**:
   - Get the Teams PC app or log in to the web app.
   - You can use Copilot in Teams on Windows, Mac, the web, Android, and iOS.

Remember that Copilot helps you be more productive and creative by giving you clever assistance in real-time.

Installation Process

1. **Install Visual Studio Code**: Get Visual Studio Code from the official page and install it if you haven't already.
2. **Open Visual Studio Code**: Open Visual Studio Code after it's been installed.
3. **Install Microsoft Copilot Extension**:
   - To get to the Extensions view in Visual Studio Code, press **Ctrl+Shift+X** or click on the square button on the left.
   - Go to the Extensions Marketplace and look for "GitHub Copilot" or "Microsoft Copilot."
   - Click the "Install" button next to the add-on for Microsoft Copilot.
4. **Authenticate with GitHub** (if required): You may need to sign in to Copilot with your GitHub account. To verify, just do what it says.
5. **Set up Copilot**: Once Copilot is installed, it may ask you to set up some options or settings. As instructed, follow the steps given.
6. **Restart Visual Studio Code** (if required): Sometimes, after installing an application, Visual Studio Code needs to be restarted. If asked, start the editor up again.
7. **Start Using Copilot**: Once Copilot is installed and set up, you should see ideas and assistance from it while you code in languages that it supports.

Integration with GitHub

It is very easy to use Microsoft Copilot with GitHub, which is the biggest site for storing and working together on code repositories in the world. By adding Copilot's AI-powered code completion and suggestion features to the GitHub environment, this integration makes it easier for developers to work on their projects. **This is how Copilot and GitHub work together:**

1. **GitHub Copilot Extension:** Visual Studio Code is one of the most famous code tools used by developers, and you can get Copilot as an add-on for it. Developers can use the Copilot extension's features right from their working environment after installing it.

2. **Code Completion and Suggestions:** When developers are writing code in VS Code and have the Copilot extension turned on, Copilot gives them intelligent code completion suggestions and code snippets that are relevant to the current situation as they write code. These ideas are made by looking at the code, the notes, and the developer's natural language explanations.

3. **GitHub Repository Integration:** To teach its AI model, Copilot uses GitHub's huge collection of open-source code. Copilot can make correct code ideas based on the computer language, libraries, and frameworks being used in a project by looking at trends and examples from GitHub repositories.

4. **GitHub Co-pilot Mode:** Copilot's connection to GitHub goes beyond just finishing code in VS Code. In its "GitHub Copilot" mode, developers can work together with Copilot right in GitHub's web-based code editor while looking through files on the site. In this mode, developers can quickly make code snippets, comment descriptions, and even whole functions right from the GitHub interface.

5. **Learning and Improvement:** The AI model keeps learning and getting better over time as developers use Copilot and follow its advice. When Copilot gives code ideas, it uses feedback from developers and ongoing study of code patterns and trends on GitHub to make them more accurate and useful.

6. **Community Feedback and Collaboration:** GitHub gives developers a place to talk about Copilot's ideas and work together to make them better. Users can directly report bugs, problems, and feature requests to the GitHub Copilot source. This lets the tool keep getting better and better.

Overall, integrating Copilot with GitHub makes it easier for developers to write code by letting them use AI-powered code completion and suggestion tools right in their work environment and GitHub repositories. This combination makes the process of writing code easier, boosts output, and encourages developers to work together.

GitHub Copilot Integration

1. **Installation:**
   - To use Copilot with GitHub, you need to add the **GitHub Copilot extension** to your code editor. Visual Studio Code currently supports this.
   - Open VS Code, press Ctrl+Shift+X to open the Extensions Marketplace, and look for "GitHub Copilot." Install the extension and follow any steps for logging in.

2. **Authentication**:
   - Once the app is installed, sign in with your GitHub account.
   - Click on the GitHub Copilot button in the sidebar of VS Code; then follow the on-screen prompts to sign in.
3. **Configuration**:
   - Click the gear button in the GitHub Copilot panel to change how Copilot works for you.
   - Change settings like language support, key bindings, and how snippets work.
4. **Usage**:
   - Open an old code project or start a new one.
   - As you write code, Copilot will make smart suggestions, complete your code automatically, and even make up whole functions based on what you're writing.
   - Press Tab or Enter to agree with Copilot's ideas.
5. **Learning and Feedback**:
   - Copilot changes as you use it and learn from the way you code.
   - If you have any problems or suggestions, you could report them through the app or the GitHub source.

Using Copilot in Various Development Environments

One of the most famous code editors used by developers, Visual Studio Code (VS Code), is built into Microsoft Copilot. However, there may be differences in how well Copilot works with other coding platforms. **Here are some ways to use Copilot in different working environments:**

1. **Visual Studio Code (VS Code):** The GitHub Copilot app makes it easy to use Copilot with VS Code. After adding the Copilot app to VS Code, you can use its features right from your code editor. As you write code in VS Code, Copilot gives you code ideas, completions, and help that is based on what you are doing.
2. **GitHub Repository:** Copilot also has a mode called "GitHub Copilot" that lets you work together with Copilot right in GitHub's web-based code editor while you're reading GitHub projects. You can make code snippets, comment descriptions, and even whole functions right from the GitHub interface when you're in this mode.
3. **Other Development Environments:** Copilot works best with VS Code and GitHub, but you might be able to use some of its features in other programming platforms as well, though not as easily. You can use Copilot's ideas by copying and pasting code snippets made in VS Code into other IDEs or tools. However, the Copilot application may not work as well in other settings as it does in VS Code because it is fully integrated and works without any problems.
4. **API and Integration Possibilities:** In the future, Copilot may be able to connect to more development platforms through APIs or connections made by outside developers, or it may be able to get official backing from GitHub and Microsoft. Keep an eye on GitHub and Microsoft's updates and news to see if anything changes in this area.

Overall, Copilot's main integrations are with VS Code and GitHub. However, developers may still be able to use its features in other development environments by copying and pasting code snippets manually or by waiting for possible future extensions and mergers.

Privacy and Security Considerations

When using any AI-powered tool, like Microsoft Copilot, you need to think about privacy and security. Microsoft protects your info with a lot of different options. Microsoft is committed to privacy, security, compliance, and responsible AI methods, and this is how all Copilot for Security data is managed. Microsoft's approved methods control who can get into the systems that store your data. **When using Copilot, here are some important things to keep in mind about privacy and safety:**

1. **Data Privacy:** To make code ideas, Copilot looks at a huge amount of code from many different sources. It was trained on public code files, but if you're working with private or sensitive code, you need to be aware of how that might affect privacy. When you use Copilot, don't give out private information or secret code.
2. **Data Security:** Make sure that your development environment is safe and up to date with the latest security changes and updates. This includes any code tools or integrated development environments (IDEs) that you use with Copilot. For added safety, this helps guard against possible security holes that bad people could use.
3. **Code Privacy:** Be careful when you use Copilot to make code snippets that could hold private data or secret methods. Before sharing the created code, make sure it is clean and free of bugs, especially if it contains private or secret logic.
4. **Access Controls:** Make sure that there are access controls in place to limit who can use Copilot and stop people from doing so without permission. If you work with other people, make sure that everyone on your team knows how to use Copilot and that only allowed team members can access it.
5. **User Consent and Transparency:** Allowing users to give permission and being clear about how their data is being used: Read and understand Copilot's data usage and privacy rules. The policies on GitHub make it clear how data is collected and used with Copilot. Users should read these policies to make smart choices about how to use the tool.
6. **Feedback and Reporting:** If you have any privacy or security worries while using Copilot, you should let GitHub or Microsoft know about them in the right way. Let the developers know about any problems or holes you find so they can make the tool safer and more private generally.
7. **Regular Updates:** Make sure you know about Copilot changes and security patches and that you're using the most recent version of the tool. Update your working environment and any software that works with it regularly to reduce security risks and get the most out of the newest features and changes.

If developers follow these privacy and security tips, they can use Microsoft Copilot effectively while reducing the risks to data privacy and security. When using Copilot or any other AI-powered tool, it's important to stay alert and take action to address any privacy or security issues that may come up.

Initial Configuration best

Making the best settings for Microsoft Copilot means making sure it's set up to improve your coding experience while also taking privacy, security, and personal tastes into account. **Here is a list of the best ways to set up Microsoft Copilot for the first time:**

1. **Install Visual Studio Code (VS Code):** Make sure that VS Code is already set up on your computer. Copilot is built into VS Code, so you need to have this code editor loaded to use Copilot's functions.

2. **Install GitHub Copilot Extension:** You can get the GitHub Copilot extension from the Visual Studio Code Marketplace and install it. To do this, press Ctrl+Shift+X to open the Extensions view and look for "GitHub Copilot." Then, choose the extension and click "Install."

3. **Sign in to GitHub:** In VS Code, sign in to your GitHub account. To get to the command line, press Ctrl+Shift+P or click on the GitHub button in the sidebar. Type "GitHub: Sign In" and then follow the on-screen instructions to log in. This step is necessary to use Copilot's features because it trains its AI model using GitHub's code sources.

4. **Configure Copilot Settings:** Copilot has several settings that you can change to make it behave the way you want it to. Click on the gear button in the bottom left corner of VS Code and choose "Settings" to get to the Copilot options. In the settings search bar, type "Copilot" to narrow down the settings that have to do with Copilot. Look over the choices and make any changes you think are necessary based on your tastes.

5. **Explore Copilot Features:** Take some time to get to know Copilot's features and what it can do. Try typing notes, code snippets, or natural language descriptions to see how Copilot helps you write code and gives you ideas. Try using Copilot in different types of writing tasks to see how it can help you get things done faster.

6. **Learn Keyboard Shortcuts:** To get more done with Copilot, learn the keyboard shortcuts that work with it. To use Copilot's ideas, press Ctrl+Space (on Windows) or Cmd+Space (on macOS).

7. **Review Privacy and Security Settings:** Check the privacy and security settings on Copilot to make sure you know how your information is being used and stored. There is clear information on GitHub about how Copilot collects and uses data, and you can check and change your privacy settings as needed.

8. **Provide Feedback:** As you use Copilot, you might want to tell GitHub and Microsoft what you think so they can make it more accurate and useful. You can give comments right in VS Code or through the feedback methods on GitHub.

By following these best practices for initial setup, you can set up Microsoft Copilot correctly and change how it works to fit your coding needs and preferences. Keep up with Copilot's updates and improvements, and make changes to your setup as needed to get the most out of your writing experience.

CHAPTER 3

UNDERSTANDING COPILOT SUGGESTIONS

1. **Input Prompt and Grounding**:
   - There is a question that you need to answer before you can use Microsoft 365 Copilot. You tell them what you need, like writing an email, making a report, or writing code for a function.
   - When you ground, the magic happens. The copilot takes your prompt and improves it by making it more detailed and aware of the situation. This process makes sure that the answers you get are useful and appropriate for your job.

2. **Privacy and Security**:
   - Copilot cares about your safety. The fact that it links to your organization's data in Microsoft 365 keeps private data safe.
   - It doesn't get to your data directly; instead, it uses Microsoft Graph to figure out what's going on. There are letters, chats, papers, and more in this group.
   - It is very important to note that the large language models (LLMs) that Copilot uses are stored in the Microsoft Cloud and were not trained on data from your company. Your privacy stays intact.

3. **Policy Adherence**:
   - The security, compliance, and privacy rules that your company sets up in Microsoft 365 are carried over to Copilot. It follows the rules!
   - Every talk starts from scratch. Your chat information is erased, so your conversations with others won't teach the LLMs anything by accident.

4. **Capabilities and Efficiency**:
   - Copilot helps you come up with answers by using the information you give it. It's like having a very smart person help you write.
   - Microsoft Search is used to help you get caught up quickly, which saves you time.
   - On top of that, Copilot reads important data from OneNote, Word, or PowerPoint files, which is a great way to start writing new content.

How Copilot Works

Advanced machine learning models, especially the GPT (Generative Pre-trained Transformer) design, are used by Microsoft Copilot to look at the context of code and make smart code ideas.

This is how Copilot works in brief:

1. **Training Data:** Copilot is learned on a huge set of code from many places, such as GitHub's open-source files. There are a lot of different computer languages, libraries, systems, and ways of writing code in this dataset. This large set of different datasets helps Copilot learn about popular code trends, idioms, and best practices.

2. **GPT Architecture:** Opening AI's GPT design is what Copilot is built on. GPT stands for "Generative Pre-trained Transformer." GPT is a cutting-edge language model that uses self-attention to understand input and write text that sounds like it was written by a person. The code-specific data that Copilot uses to fine-tune its model makes it very good at understanding and making code samples.

3. **Contextual Understanding:** When you write code or natural language descriptions in your code editor, Copilot looks at the variable names, function signatures, notes, and other code snippets that are nearby. It uses this knowledge of the context to come up with useful code ideas that fit the current coding situation.

4. **Code Completion and Generation:** As you type, Copilot gives you ideas for how to finish off function names, variable names, method calls, and other types of code depending on what you are doing. Also, Copilot can make whole pieces of code based on notes or natural language descriptions from the coder. The patterns and structures learned from the training data are used to make these bits of code.

5. **Machine Learning Models:** The machine learning models in Copilot are always learning and changing based on how users interact with them and what they say. The models get smarter as developers use Copilot and add its ideas to their code. Over time, these interactions help the models make better predictions. This process of learning over and over again helps Copilot get better at suggesting code and being accurate about it.

6. **Privacy and Security:** Because of worries about privacy and security, Copilot works in a way that protects privacy. It doesn't send or keep user data or bits of code outside of the local development area. Copilot's training data comes from code repositories that are open to the public. Unless the user directly tells it to, it doesn't view or examine private or sensitive code.

For the most part, Microsoft Copilot uses machine learning to understand the context of code, make smart code suggestions, and help developers write code more quickly. It is a useful tool for improving the writing experience because it can look at different coding styles and change based on how the user interacts with it.

How does Microsoft Copilot for Microsoft 365 work?

The features of Microsoft Copilot for Microsoft 365 that users see in Microsoft 365 Apps and other places look like smart features, functions, and the ability to remind users. The foundation **LLMs and Microsoft-only technologies work together to make a system that lets you view, use, and control your organization's data safely.**

- **Microsoft 365 Apps** like Word, Excel, PowerPoint, Outlook, Teams, and Loop work with Copilot for Microsoft 365 to help users with their work. For instance, Word's Copilot feature is meant to help users create, read, and edit papers. For the same reason, Copilot in the other apps helps users with their work in those apps.
- **Microsoft Copilot with Graph-grounded chat** lets you use work-related material and context in chats in Microsoft Copilot. You can draft content, catch up on what you missed,

and get answers to questions through open-ended prompts with Graph-grounded chat, all while keeping your work data safe.

- **Microsoft Graph** has been an important part of Microsoft 365 for a long time. There is information about how users, actions, and your organization's records are connected. If you use the Microsoft Graph API, you can add more information from customer signs like emails, chats, papers, and meetings to the prompt.
- **Semantic Index** for Copilot uses several LLMs that sit on top of Microsoft Graph to understand user questions and give you smart, useful, and international answers that make you more productive. You can quickly look through billions of vectors, which are mathematical representations of features or characteristics, to find information that is useful to your company.

Looking at the image below will help you understand how Microsoft Copilot for Microsoft 365 works.

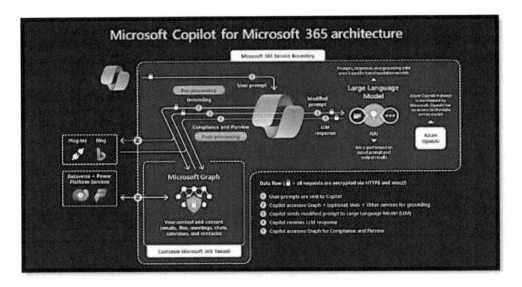

To explain how Microsoft Copilot for Microsoft 365 works, read on:

- A user may ask Copilot to do something in an app like Word or PowerPoint.
- Additionally, Copilot pre-processes the input prompt using a method called "grounding," which makes the prompt more specific. This helps you get replies that are relevant and useful for your job. The prompt can have text from input files or other content that Copilot finds. It is then sent to the LLM to be processed. Copilot can only view data that a specific person already has access to, for example, because of role-based access controls in Microsoft 365.

- After getting the answer from the LLM, Copilot processes it. Other calls to Microsoft Graph for grounding, responsible AI checks, security, compliance, privacy reviews, and command creation are all part of this post-processing.
- Copilot sends the answer back to the app so the user can look it over and decide what to do with it.

How does Copilot work with Each Microsoft Application?

Copilot is a powerful tool that is meant to work as smoothly as possible with other Microsoft products. It helps users get things done and is smart enough to do it for them. This is how Copilot works with some well-known Microsoft programs:

Copilot in Word

Copilot in Word changes the way you write quickly and creatively. You can use it to create, summarize, understand, improve, and raise your documents. You can now use better features, such as seeing and turning text into a table, adding to existing questions, writing a document by mentioning up to three documents and finding information about your document.

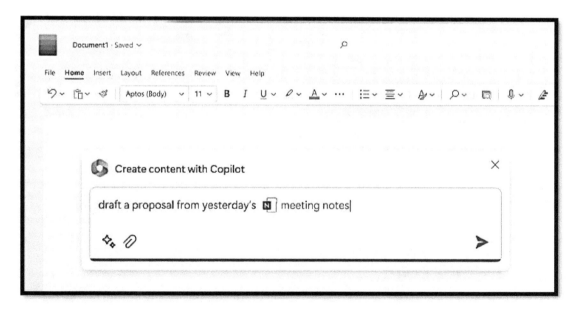

Copilot makes it easy to write a first draft by giving you ideas and building on what you've already written. Using Copilot's editing tools, you can easily turn the text into tables. Start a conversation with Copilot to get more information that will help and improve your work. If you're short on time, Copilot can recap your doc for you.

Copilot in Excel

In Excel, Copilot works with you to help you look at and evaluate your data. Use real words, not just formulas, to ask Copilot questions about your information. Your questions will cause it to find connections, come up with what-if scenarios, and suggest new formulas. These models will help you explore your data without changing it. To get different results, look for trends, make powerful graphics, or ask for advice.

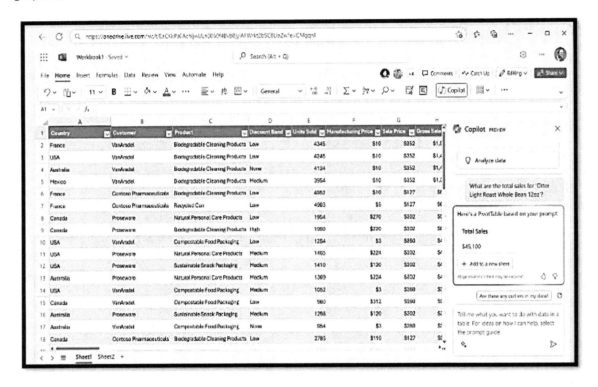

You can use Copilot to help you explore and understand your data better. Easily find the most important results and see your data in a way that makes sense. You can quickly highlight, filter, and sort your data so you can focus on what's important. Copilot's ideas for complex math make it easy to come up with formulas.

Copilot in PowerPoint

Copilot in PowerPoint helps you make slideshows that look great. Copilot can take written papers that you already have and turn them into decks with speaker notes and sources. It can also help you start a new presentation from a simple prompt or plan.

You can tell Copilot what to write about and it will make a rough draft of your talk. Copilot has what you need whether you're making a new presentation or just need a quick rundown of a longer one. Let Copilot put your slides in order and easily rearrange them the way you want. Plus, Copilot can make slides or pictures that are customized with your organization's logo.

Copilot in Outlook

Outlook's Copilot feature helps you stay on top of your email and send powerful messages in much less time.

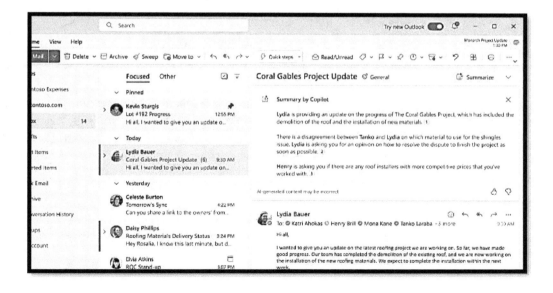

You can turn long email talks into short recaps with Copilot. You can now ask Copilot to recap an email thread so that you can quickly get to the original message and get ideas for answers, action items, and follow-up meetings. When writing an email, you can also pick the length and tone.

Copilot in Teams

This feature in Teams called "Copilot" lets you easily summarize talks, carefully organize important points of discussion, and make meeting plans based on chat history.

During a meeting, you can summarize important points of the talk and suggest things that should be done. Get answers to specific questions and catch up on any information you may have missed to stay informed. This clever tool also makes it easier to find people to follow up with and makes it easy to schedule follow-up meetings. This improves your team's contact and leads to more work getting done.

Copilot in Viva

The cutting-edge AI tool in Microsoft Viva is called Copilot. It gives you quick, accurate, and customized answers and insights that are relevant to your business.

Conversational AI in Viva Goals' Copilot makes it easy to set and improve goals. Next-generation AI is used by Microsoft Viva Copilot to speed up worker insights and boost employee involvement. It gives management predictive tools that help them build a more connected and productive staff. Copilot protects privacy, security, and compliance while encouraging responsible AI use and higher employee involvement.

Copilot in OneNote

OneNote's Copilot feature can help you change and organize your plan, so you can stay more organized and take action from your notes.

Let Copilot take your notes and turn them into doable to-do lists. You can now get more out of your notes by asking more in-depth questions, summarizing your content, or asking Copilot to create content for you. It can also help you write more clearly.

Copilot in Loop

Copilot in Loop lets you use the power of shared thought to co-create, catch up, and stay on the same page with your team.

Use the ideas that Copilot gives you to get what you want in Microsoft Loop. You can now use Copilot as a team to make changes together. You can co-create prompts and tables to help organize team projects, pick up where your coworkers left off, summarize page content, and make a recap for a partner you are giving work.

Copilot in Whiteboard

Copilot in Whiteboard helps you get your brainstorming process going and speed it up so you can come up with, sort, and describe your ideas faster.

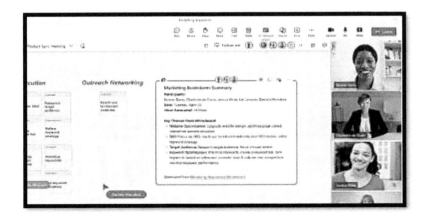

Copilot can describe complicated whiteboards, which makes it easy to share notes with Microsoft Loop. Work with other people, get feedback from Copilot on what you're making and turn your brainstorming session into a finished show.

Microsoft Copilot in Team Communication

Microsoft Copilot is a key part of changing how teams talk to each other, making exchanges more streamlined to improve teamwork and productivity.

Facilitating Effective Communication

With its advanced AI features, Microsoft Copilot improves team communication by cutting down on mistakes and making things clearer.

- **Automated Meeting Summaries**: After a team meeting, Copilot can write short recaps that include the main points, choices made, and things that need to be done. This keeps everyone in sync, even if they can't make it to the meeting.
- **Action Item Tracking:** The copilot keeps track of action items from communications and meetings, giving notes to those responsible to make sure they follow through and making the team more accountable.
- **Real-time Language Translation**: It's easy for people from different countries to work together when Copilot's real-time translation breaks down language obstacles. For example, a team from Germany, Japan, and the USA could work together on a project without any problems because Copilot would translate all messages in real-time, making sure that everyone on the team understood all emails, meeting minutes, and project reports.

Automating Routine Communication Tasks

By automating routine conversations, Microsoft Copilot cuts down on the time needed for administrative tasks by a large amount.

- **Scheduling Meetings**: Copilot can easily find times that work for everyone on the team, taking into account their different time zones, and send out invites. This saves time that would have been spent back and forth setting up meetings.
- **Organizing Email Communications**: It can sort new emails by importance and write answers to common questions ahead of time, which makes managing emails easier and saves time.

This kind of technology has huge effects. One project team at a marketing firm said that after using Copilot, their routine costs went down by 30%. This gave them more time to work on strategic tasks like planning campaigns and keeping clients engaged.

Enhancing Team Dynamics and Productivity

Adding AI-powered communication tools like Microsoft Copilot changes the way teams work together and how much they get done.

- **Increased Transparency**: automated reports and tracking make sure that everyone on the team has access to the same data, which builds trust and openness.
- **Faster Decision-Making**: Teams can make better decisions more quickly with the help of AI-driven insights and data analysis, which cuts down on project timelines.
- **More Inclusive Participation**: Tools like real-time translation and meeting reports make sure that everyone on the team can fully participate in team processes, no matter where they live or how well they speak the language.

A software development business that used Microsoft Copilot as part of its process is an interesting case study. Project finish times got a lot faster for the company, and team happiness went through the roof. The team was able to focus on development work because they could quickly send out project updates and action items and had fewer administrative jobs to do. This led to a 40% increase in total productivity.

Boosting Project Management with Microsoft Copilot

Microsoft Copilot is changing the way projects are managed by adding AI-powered accuracy and speed to old ways of doing things.

Streamlining Project Management

Microsoft Copilot changes the way projects are managed by making the planning and performance steps easier and better.

- **Data Analysis and Optimization**: This part looks at project data to predict possible delays and suggest ways to speed up work processes so that projects go easily and don't run into any problems that aren't necessary.
- **Predicting Bottlenecks**: Copilot lets you make changes ahead of time to keep things moving along and on schedule by predicting bottlenecks before they happen.

One important use is for managing complicated software development tasks. Copilot looks at past data to find common problems in the development process and offers changes ahead of time, like moving resources around or changing deadlines, which makes project performance much smoother.

Task Delegation and Progress Tracking

Microsoft Copilot shines when it comes to intelligently delegating tasks and keeping an eye on how projects are going in real-time.

- **Intelligent Task Delegation**: Copilot gives tasks to team members by looking at their skills, experience, and present workload. This makes sure that everyone is responsible for the right amount of work.
- **Real-time Progress Monitoring**: It keeps a close eye on project timelines and resource sharing, giving real-time reports on progress and pointing out areas that need more work.

Copilot was used by an engineering company to oversee a big building project. By using Copilot's features for delegating tasks and keeping track of progress, the company was able to cut the time it took to finish a project by 20% and make all team members happier by distributing work more fairly.

Case Studies in Project Management

Real-life examples of how Microsoft Copilot has changed the way projects are managed and how well they get done show how powerful it is.

- **Time Savings and Cost Reduction**: As a result, a global marketing firm cut costs and saved time by adding Copilot to its project management system. Project finish times were cut by 25%, and routine costs were cut by 15%, thanks to better job allocation and resource use.
- **Enhanced Team Coordination**: After using Copilot, a tech company said that team coordination and project results got a lot better. The platform's predictive analytics and real-time reports helped the team manage a complicated product launch with many

moving parts. The result was a successful, on-time release that went above and beyond what stakeholders expected.

Microsoft Copilot for Collaborative Creativity and Problem-Solving

Teams can use Microsoft Copilot to work together and solve problems in new and creative ways.

- **Facilitating Creative Brainstorming:**

Talk about how Copilot can be used to help people come up with ideas, creative solutions, and data-driven insights during discussion meetings. Stress that it can provide different points of view and create fake thinking situations to encourage creation.

- **Leveraging AI for Problem-Solving:**

Look into how Copilot's AI-powered research can help teams find issues, think about possible answers, and guess what will happen. Show how Copilot can look at huge amounts of data and come up with ideas that help solve hard problems.

- **Fostering a Collaborative Environment:**

Give examples of how to use Microsoft Copilot to encourage teamwork and clear communication. Advice on how to use Copilot so that it improves teamwork instead of taking its place.

Integrating Microsoft Copilot into Existing Workflow Tools

Adding Microsoft Copilot to current teamwork and workflow tools can make things run much more smoothly and efficiently. How well this connection works is very important for getting the most out of Copilot without messing up existing processes.

Best Practices for Integration

Seamless Integration with Collaboration Platforms: If you want to combine Microsoft Copilot with Microsoft Teams, Asana, or Slack, you need to plan so that Copilot works with the other platform instead of on top of it.

- **Enhance, Don't Duplicate:** Make sure that Copilot's features add value to other tools without copying features. Instead, focus on areas that need to be automated or improved.
- **Customize Interactions:** Change the settings for Copilot to fit the way you communicate and handle projects on each platform, whether you're using Asana for official reports or Slack for more casual updates.

Integrating Copilot with Microsoft Teams is a good example of how to make meeting scheduling and minutes more automated. This saves project manager's time and makes the team more productive.

Tailoring Copilot Functionality

By changing how Copilot works, you can make it fit your team's specific process needs.

- **Automating Routine Updates**: Set up Copilot to handle regular progress reports in project management tools. This will free up team members to work on more important tasks.
- **Facilitating Data Collection**: You can set up Copilot to collect and combine data from different sources, so you don't have to manually put together reports.

One way that Copilot was changed to fit the routine of a development team was by automating sprint retrospectives. Copilot gathered comments from individuals through Slack, put it all together, and presented it in a structured way during sprint review talks. This made the review process much better.

Ensuring Seamless Integration

Making it easy for Copilot to fit into current processes is important for both its usefulness and its popularity among users.

- **Phased Rollouts**: Put Copilot into use slowly so that teams can get used to the new features without being too overwhelmed.
- **Continuous Feedback Loops**: Set up ways for users to give feedback on how well Copilot works and how well it integrates with other apps. This will help the app keep getting better.
- **Training and Support**: Make sure that everyone on the team is comfortable and skilled with Copilot's features and knows how to use them with other tools by giving them thorough training lessons.

For integration to go well, it's important to focus on user acceptance through ease of use and show clear benefits. As an example, a marketing firm added Copilot to the way they made content. The team learned how to use Copilot within their current workflow in Trello through focused training meetings. This made the content approval process run more smoothly and helped them finish the project on time.

Basic Commands and Functions

Microsoft Copilot works perfectly with Visual Studio Code (VS Code) because it is an application that is built in. Copilot doesn't have standard "commands" or "functions" as stand-alone software does, but it does have many features and functions that can be reached through keyboard shortcuts, code interactions, and ideas that are based on the current situation.

Some simple things you can do with Microsoft Copilot are listed below:

1. **Code Completion:** As you type code in VS Code, Copilot gives you smart ideas for how to finish the line based on what you're typing. You can press Tab or Enter to accept an idea, or you can use the arrow keys to move through the options.
2. **Generating Code Snippets:** Copilot can make whole pieces of code snippets based on coder notes or natural language descriptions. To make a code snippet, just type a short explanation of what you want to do in plain text or as a comment, and Copilot will make suggestions based on what you type.
3. **Keyboard Shortcuts:** You can use keyboard shortcuts to call up Copilot and start certain tasks or conversations. Even though Copilot doesn't have instructions, you can use the VS Code interface and keyboard shortcuts to get to its functions. For instance, you can use Ctrl+Space or Cmd+Space to bring up Copilot ideas.
4. **Contextual Assistance:** Copilot gives you contextual help based on the variable names, function labels, and other code snippets around them. It looks at the code's style and structure to give you ideas and completions that make sense in this particular case.
5. **Learning and Adaptation:** Copilot is always learning and changing based on how users connect with it and what they say. When you use Copilot and add its ideas to your code, it learns from these interactions and improves its models so that it can make better suggestions in the future.

6. **Feedback and Reporting:** If Copilot gives you errors or ideas that aren't the best, you can let it know so it can get better at what it does. You can give comments right in VS Code or through the feedback methods on GitHub.
7. **Privacy and Security Controls:** Copilot protects your privacy, and you can look at and change its privacy and security options as required. In your local work environment, you can control who can use Copilot and make sure that your data is treated safely.

Copilot doesn't have any orders or functions that work on their own, but it does have a lot of tools and options that are meant to make coding in VS Code better. When engineers use its clever code completion, code generation, and contextual help, they can write code faster and better.

Mastering the User Interface and Navigation

We made the Copilot interface to be simple and easy to use, and it works with all of your other Microsoft 365 apps without any problems.

You can use the following steps to get to the Copilot tools in different M365 apps:

Word, Excel, and PowerPoint: You can get to Copilot in Word, Excel, and PowerPoint through the command bar and window. This is where you can make requests, see ideas, and make changes directly to your document, spreadsheet, or presentation.

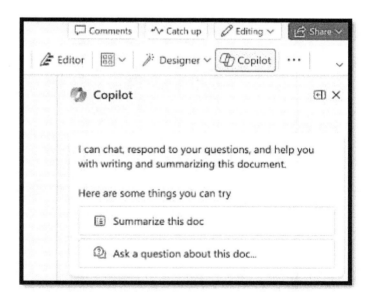

Outlook: You can turn on Copilot in the email writing window to help you come up with content based on the email's context or the recipient's details.

Teams: Team members can use the Copilot features to get help and work together in real-time during meetings or chats.

OneNote, Loop, and Whiteboard, Forms: Copilot is built into writing and creation tools like OneNote, Loop, Whiteboard, and Forms. It gives you ideas and help as you work on your projects.

When you first start using Copilot, it's helpful to get used to a few simple tasks and features:

- **Ask questions:** Type a question or request in normal words, and Copilot will answer or do something. Like "Summarize the most important parts of this document" in Word.
- **Create drafts:** Give Copilot a short description of what you need and ask it to write emails, papers, or slideshows.
- **Summarize content:** Copilot can quickly highlight the most important parts of long emails, papers, or slideshows when summarizing content.

Generating Code with Copilot

Using Copilot in Visual Studio Code, you can add AI-generated code that will help you write code by letting you chat in normal language. You can change things about a site in Power Pages using HTML, JS, or CSS code, which isn't possible in the Power Pages low-code design workshop right now. This Copilot chat experience helps Power Pages developers like you write code by using normal language to describe how you want the code to work. The code that was made can then be improved and used to make changes to your site. When you use Microsoft Copilot to generate code, it uses its AI-powered features to give you smart code ideas and snippets based on notes or descriptions written in natural language.

In Visual Studio Code, here's how to use Copilot to write code:

1. **Install Copilot Extension:** Make sure that the GitHub Copilot extension is present in Visual Studio Code. If you look for "GitHub Copilot" in the Visual Studio Code Marketplace, you can find the app and install it.
2. **Sign in to GitHub:** To use Copilot's functions, sign in to your GitHub account in Visual Studio Code. You can either click on the GitHub button in the sidebar or press Ctrl+Shift+P to bring up the command panel and run the "GitHub: Sign In" command.
3. **Activate Copilot:** Copilot should be on by default once you're logged in. You can start using the tools of Copilot while writing code in Visual Studio Code.
4. **Generate Code Snippets:** You can give Copilot high-level details or comments about the features you want to add to produce code snippets. For instance, if you want to add a method that finds the factorial of a number, you could write a comment like this: # Find the factorial of a number. Your response will be read by Copilot, which will then create code snippets that do what you stated. To use the code that was created, all you have to do is accept Copilot's offer.
5. **Provide Context:** Copilot can only make code snippets if your code and notes give it some background. When you talk about the features you need, be as specific and detailed as you can. The more information you give, the more correct and useful the code snippets that are created will be.

6. **Review and Modify Suggestions:** Once Copilot makes code suggestions, you should look them over to make sure they meet your needs and follow coding standards. You might need to change or adapt the code snippets that are created to fit your needs or the way you normally write code.

7. **Incorporate Generated Code:** It's possible to add created code to your codebase once you're happy with the code snippets that were produced. Copilot's ideas are made to work with your current code, so it's easy to add AI-generated features to your projects and make them better.

8. **Provide Feedback:** If Copilot gives you wrong or less-than-ideal code ideas, you can give feedback to help it get better at what it does. You can give feedback right in Visual Studio Code or through the feedback methods on GitHub.

By doing these things, you can use the AI-powered features of Microsoft Copilot to make code snippets quickly and easily in Visual Studio Code. This will help you be more productive as a coder.

Code Completion and Suggestions

Copilot is great at completing code in real-time. As you type, it makes smart suggestions based on the computer language and framework you've chosen. This tool not only helps you code faster, but it also makes sure that your work is correct. Some of the most important features of Microsoft Copilot are code completion and tips, which are meant to help developers write code faster.

Let me show you how code completion and ideas work in Copilot:

1. **Contextual Suggestions:** As you type code in Visual Studio Code (VS Code), Copilot gives you ideas that are relevant to what you are typing. The programming language, libraries, frameworks, and code snippets you're using, along with the suggestions, are all taken into account.

2. **Variable Names and Function Calls:** As you type, Copilot offers variable names, function names, method calls, and other code elements to help you finish them fast and correctly. These ideas come from best practices and general trends found in the data that Copilot's AI model learned from.

3. **Method Signatures and Parameters:** When you call functions or methods, Copilot suggests method signatures and parameter lists, which may include input names and default values. This helps you quickly add the right arguments to method or function calls.

4. **Error Correction and Validation:** Copilot can help you find and fix mistakes in your code by offering different pieces of code or pointing out grammar mistakes. It can also check your code against common coding rules and practices and give you suggestions for how to make it better or more efficient.

5. **Code Snippets and Templates:** These are short pieces of code and templates that Copilot provides for common computing jobs and patterns. You can use these snippets to quickly build code without having to start from scratch. They can be anything from simple phrases to whole functions or classes.

6. **Natural Language Descriptions:** Copilot can get code snippets based on natural language descriptions or notes given by the developer, in addition to standard code completion. You can use plain English to describe the features you need, and Copilot will figure out what you mean and suggest code that will make those features work.

7. **Learning and Adaptation:** Copilot is always learning and changing based on how users connect with it and what they say. When you use Copilot and add its ideas to your code, it learns from these interactions and improves its models so that it can make better suggestions in the future.

8. **Integration with Development Workflow:** Copilot works with VS Code's development process without any problems, giving ideas and completions right in the code editor. It's easy to add Copilot's ideas to your code because you can accept them with a single click.

Overall, Microsoft Copilot's code completion and ideas are meant to improve the coding experience by giving developers smart, context-aware help that lets them write code more quickly and correctly.

Contextual Understanding

Copilot uses Microsoft Graph to learn more about the context of a person, their past contacts, and organizational data. This knowledge of the context makes sure that the material that is generated is useful and fits with what the user wants. Contextual understanding is an important part of how Microsoft Copilot works. It refers to Copilot's ability to understand the situation in which code is being written and offer smart ideas and completions that are appropriate for that situation.

In Microsoft Copilot, this is how contextual understanding works:

1. **Code Context Analysis:** As you type in your code editor (like Visual Studio Code), Copilot looks at the code environment in real-time. To figure out what's going on in the code, it looks at things like variable names, function labels, notes, and other code snippets nearby.

2. **Syntax and Semantics:** Copilot reads the code and figures out what it means by figuring out its syntax and semantics. It finds patterns, connections, and dependencies in the code so that it can give you correct ideas and completions that follow the syntax and meaning of the computer language.

3. **Language and Library Awareness:** Copilot knows what computer language you're using and what libraries or tools are in your project. It uses this information to give language-specific ideas and completions, such as function names, method signatures, and APIs that are special to a library.

4. **Code Patterns and Best Practices:** Copilot learns from a huge set of code from many places, such as GitHub's open-source libraries. From this information, it learns common coding patterns, idioms, and best practices, which it then uses to make ideas and complete sentences that make sense.

5. **Natural Language Interaction:** Copilot can read natural language notes or descriptions from developers in addition to studying the context of the code. You can use plain English

to describe the features you need, and Copilot will make code snippets that match your description while also taking into account the other codes around them.

6. **Real-time Feedback:** Copilot understands of context changes based on how users interact with it and the feedback it receives. Copilot learns from your actions and improves its models so it can make better suggestions in the future. It does this by letting you accept or reject its ideas and adding them to your code.

7. **Accuracy and Relevance:** Copilot's contextual understanding is meant to give correct and useful ideas and completions that help developers write code more quickly and correctly. Copilot's goal is to provide clever help that fits the developer's needs and goals by looking at the context of the code being written.

Overall, knowing the context is a key part of Microsoft Copilot's AI-powered features. This lets it offer smart code ideas and completions that are tailored to the current coding situation, language, and libraries being used.

CHAPTER 4

ADVANCED FEATURES OF MICROSOFT COPILOT

Microsoft Copilot has more advanced tools than just the ability to complete code and make suggestions. With these tools, developers can get more help and get more done with artificial intelligence.

The following are some of Microsoft Copilot's more powerful features:

1. **Code Generation from Comments:** Copilot can make code based on comments or natural language statements that the coder gives it. Developers can tell Copilot to write the necessary code by leaving a note that describes the desired feature in plain English.
2. **Refactoring Suggestions:** Copilot can make ideas for rewriting code, such as making it faster, easier to read, or more in line with best practices. It can find places in code that can be refactored and offer ways to make things better.
3. **Error Detection and Correction:** Copilot can help you find and fix mistakes in your code by suggesting different pieces of code or calling out grammar mistakes. It can look at the context of the code to find possible problems and give advice on how to fix them.
4. **Complex Code Completion:** Copilot can handle complex coding situations and offer smart code completions for advanced language features like functional programming, asynchronous programming, generics, and more.
5. **Integration with Git Version Control:** Copilot works with Git version control without any problems, so developers can use Visual Studio Code to interact with their Git files. This integration lets you do things like commit changes, push and pull code, fix merge issues, and see the past of commits.
6. **Enhanced Code Understanding:** Copilot is always learning from how users interact with it and what they say, so it can better understand code context, language meanings, and coding trends. Over time, it can change to different ways of writing code, organizing projects, and working with developers.
7. **Customization and Configuration:** Copilot lets you change how it works to fit your needs and the needs of your project. To get the most out of Copilot, developers can change settings for code ideas, privacy, security, and more.
8. **Cross-Language Support:** Copilot works with many computer languages and can make smart ideas and complete code in many languages and frameworks. It can switch between languages in a project without any problems and provide language-specific help when needed.
9. **Code Snippet Expansion:** Depending on the information given, Copilot can turn code snippets into fully made applications. With this tool, developers can quickly add templates, boilerplate code, or common patterns without having to write them manually.

10. **Feedback Mechanisms:** Copilot wants comments from users to make it more accurate and useful. Developers can report problems, suggest changes, or make general comments through Visual Studio Code's feedback channels or GitHub's feedback channels.

All of these advanced features make developers more productive and improve their coding experience by giving them smart help, automation, and insights throughout the development process.

Exploring Extensively Large Language

AI is changing the world, and large language models (LLMs) are at the center of this change, especially in apps like Copilot for Microsoft 365. These models stand out because they can understand and write text that sounds like it was written by a person. In LLMs, the word "large" means two different things. Before anything else, it refers to the size of the models, which include a lot of different factors. Second, it refers to the huge amounts of data that these models are taught on. Because they are both broad and deep, LLMs can understand language details and complexities better than AI models that are only broad. LLMs are what make Copilot for Microsoft 365 work. They make a lot of features possible that change the way people use technology. These LLMs, which are hosted on Microsoft's Azure OpenAI Service, let Copilot process and react to user inputs in a way that looks and feels like talking to a person. To do this, you need to understand the details of what users are asking for and come up with answers that are perfect for each case. One of the most important things that Copilot does is use these LLMs to make the work experience better for users. By connecting to different Microsoft 365 apps, Copilot can make smart, situational suggestions and tips that increase efficiency and productivity.

Copilot's use of LLMs makes sure that help is always available, knowing and meeting users' needs automatically, whether they are writing an email in Outlook, making a document in Word, or getting ready for a show in PowerPoint. A lot of care is also taken to protect privacy and data security when LLMs are used in Copilot. Microsoft makes sure that even though Copilot uses LLMs to make it more useful, it also follows all privacy rules and data protection guidelines. This balance is very important for keeping users' trust, especially now that data security is so important. To sum up, Large Language Models play many roles in Copilot for Microsoft 365. They let Copilot understand and write text that sounds like it was written by a person, and they make user contact easy, quick, and safe. By adding LLMs to Copilot, a big step has been taken toward making AI apps that are smarter and more useful for people.

What is the Large Language Model's Role in Copilot for Microsoft 365?

- **The core of Language Capabilities:** LLMs take user input and write human-like writing that makes sense in the given situation.
- **Understanding and Response Generation:** They figure out what the user is asking and write the right answers.

- **Foundation for AI Interactions:** LLMs are a key part of Copilot's smart interaction with Microsoft 365 apps.
- **Enhancing User Experience:** Their advanced language processing makes users much more efficient and productive.

Natural Language Processing (NLP) in Copilot for Microsoft 365

NLP: Bridging Human and Machine Language

Natural Language Processing (NLP) is one of the most important parts of Copilot for Microsoft 365. It connects human words to machine understanding. NLP helps Copilot read and understand writing like a person would, and it comes up with answers that are natural and make sense. This technology is very important for turning complicated human language into a form that computers can understand and process. This makes sure that exchanges with Copilot are smooth and quick.

Key NLP Components

- **Tokenization:** This process breaks text into smaller pieces, like words or phrases. This simplicity is important for AI to understand, and it makes it easier for Copilot to read and process information. By breaking words down into tokens, Copilot can better understand the structure and meaning of what users are typing, which leads to more accurate answers.
- **Semantic Analysis:** To understand language, you need to know what it means and how it fits into the world. Copilot can read more than just the words in a text because semantic analysis helps it understand what the text means. This understanding is important for Copilot to help you in all of your Microsoft 365 apps in a way that is useful and aware of your situation.
- **Sentiment Analysis:** Copilot uses sentiment analysis to figure out how someone feels about something written down.

This analysis helps us understand what the person was trying to do better. For example, Copilot can change the tone and nature of its answer depending on whether the user's request is pressing or not. This makes the interaction more personalized and useful.

- **Language Translation:** Copilot can help people who speak different languages because it uses NLP to translate between them. In today's globalized job climate, this feature is particularly useful. It lets Copilot get around language obstacles and make it easier for people of different languages to talk to each other in Microsoft 365 apps.

Models Incorporating Copilot with Microsoft Graph

Microsoft Graph is the structure that connects all of the Microsoft 365 services and data. It's what makes Copilot for Microsoft 365 work, and it lets it find and combine information from many sources in a user's tenant.

- **Unifying Data Sources:** Graph brings together data from services like Outlook, OneDrive, SharePoint, Teams, and more, creating a single pool of data that Copilot can use.
- **Context-Rich Information:** By combining data from these different sources, Copilot can get a lot of context, which makes its answers more relevant and correct.

Contextual and Secure Data Access

Microsoft Graph not only combines data, but it also makes sure that the data that Copilot for Microsoft 365 can access meets the strictest security and safety standards.

- **Compliance and Security:** When Copilot talks to Microsoft Graph, it follows strict security measures and compliance rules. This makes sure that answers are based on information the user can see.
- **Role-Based Access Controls:** The Microsoft Graph API is very important for keeping role-based access controls up to date. This makes sure that the answers from Copilot for Microsoft 365 are safe and follow company rules.

Utilizing the strengths of Microsoft Graph, Copilot for Microsoft 365 can provide a smooth, safe, and tightly connected user experience across all Microsoft 365 apps. Adding this feature makes Copilot more useful and efficient, and it makes sure that user data is treated carefully and in line with company and government rules.

Utilizing Copilot for Sophisticated Data Analysis

It is the copilot's job to help the pilot navigate the plane, follow procedures, carry out orders, and give the captain corrects information right away so that the captain can make choices that are safe for the flight. Think about the role of First Officer Jeff Skiles played by Aaron Eckhart in the movie "Sully." When their plane has problems, he jumps into action right away to help Captain Sullenberger by giving him data, running checklists, checking different states, and helping the captain make an important choice in any way he can. Real-life boardrooms aren't too far behind when it comes to having to act quickly under a lot of stress. Business leaders also need a copilot to help them handle high-stakes scenarios, handle crises right away, spot possible red flags ahead of time, and work quickly. Copilots for Data Analytics meet this need and make sure that business leaders can make decisions and do their daily work without any problems.

What is a copilot for data analytics? How do copilots impact data analytics?

A copilot for Data Analytics is an artificial intelligence (AI) assistant that helps users automate time-consuming manual tasks, talk to enterprise data in simple terms, find actionable insights and present them in narratives that are easy to understand, and make the information experience more personal. Generative AI, Natural Language Processing (NLP), Machine Learning (ML), and Large Language Models (LLMs) are all strong tools that the AI copilot uses to get ideas and share them. A copilot for data analytics is a skilled data analyst, a personal business assistant, an always-available guide, the main person who makes things possible, and an engaging assistant. It's been a long time since data analytics was only for technical researchers. Now, non-technical business users are encouraged to do their analytics. Copilots make data analytics even easier by making data easier to find, data queries easier to understand, and findings easier to use and put into action. Users can ask questions like "Why did demand for Product ABC rise in Q1?" and get answers right away in the form of text descriptions and best-fit images. There are more and more AI copilots being used in fields other than data analytics. As an example, GitHub Copilot, Amazon CodeWhisperer, and Microsoft Copilot have all been shown to be useful for creating and reviewing code, making code and writing ideas, and creating texts and content assets to help users be more productive and make fewer mistakes. A study by GitHub found that developers who used GitHub copilot were 30% more productive. Copilots have been used in many fields to speed up the finishing of work, save mental energy that would have been used on repeated tasks, and make workers happier and more focused at work.

Maximizing data analytics efficiency by leveraging copilot's dynamic features

From getting the data ready to generating insights, a copilot for data analytics speeds up the process of getting useful information from unstructured data. This makes the jobs of data engineers and researchers easier and gives business users more control over their information needs. Here are some of the ways that copilot's features help make data analytics more efficient:

Curate and enrich data automatically

Copilot can help improve business data by adding synonyms, making useful labels for data rows and columns, finding connections between them, and cataloging and organizing data so that it can be analyzed effectively and correctly.

Provide suggestions to improve quality

The quality of ideas is directly related to the quality of the data. Copilots can report on the quality of data and make ideas for how to make it better in terms of being full, clear, readable, consistent, and correct.

Ask questions in simple language

Users don't have to deal with hard grammar and SQL searches to get information. Copilot lets users ask questions directly to their business data using natural language and easy-to-use tools. Copilots can also automatically make search ideas based on business data, which makes the search process easier. Everyone in a company can now receive data and insights thanks to this.

Leverage LLMs to parse human language queries better

People's language is full of jargon, slang, unplanned sentences, non-standard spelling, and words that can mean different things in different situations. Copilots use the benefits of LLMs to understand natural language questions, find the right context to give useful information and get rid of irrelevant content.

Create narratives and audio-visual data stories

It is faster and easier for data analytics copilots to make insight tales, written summaries, audiovisual data stories, live presentations, and interesting graphics. Users can easily understand business situations, share and show summed-up results in a better way, and feel sure in their decisions when they use these automatically generated content formats.

Provide tailored insights and business headlines

Copilots can make suggestions and insights that are relevant to the user by looking at their past searches, usage habits, hobbies, business metrics, and the searches they have already done. They can also get rid of data that isn't useful. Business headlines can be programmed to come up with and share ideas without people having to look for them.

Who can benefit from using Copilot for data analytics?

Many user roles in a company can use data analytics copilots to make their work more productive and efficient.

Data Engineers and Stewards

Copilots help data engineers and data stewards clean, organize, and get the business data ready. By simplifying manual, time-consuming, and repeating tasks, copilots can process data more quickly, find and fix problems more quickly, and free up the data teams to work on new ideas and more difficult tasks.

Data Scientists and Analysts

Copilots help data scientists and analysts find connections in large amounts of data and better organize it to make it more useful, make business language easier to understand, and give data more meaning by creating automatic words, names that are easy to remember, and descriptions that make sense. Copilots help analysts make sure that accurate data is always available for analysis by finding problems with the quality of the data and suggesting ways to fix them.

Business Users

Business users like product managers, sales reps, finance officers, marketing leaders, and customer success agents can use copilots to ask questions about data in a natural way, get real-time insights, and get personalized suggestions. Copilot also lets business users make dynamic screens and results on their own. Copilots help users understand insights faster and better by making recaps of key results, audiovisual data stories, and bite-sized insights.

Potential use cases for copilot in data analytics

Here are some ways that copilots can improve business processes across organizations, with AI-powered analytics giving them more information and helping them make better choices:

Sales

By asking natural language questions, sales managers can quickly compare sales across many dimensions, such as periods, regions, products, and customer groups. They can also find out which products have the highest profit margins, which products have the most popular products and any other sales changes that don't make sense. Getting answers right away can help them keep an eye on sales, figure out where growth is slowing or speeding up, and move right away.

Banking

A copilot for data analytics lets bankers ask simple questions like "loans disbursed in Q1", "what is the percentage of high net-worth customers", "Compare the deposits from 2018 to 204", and "By how much did the savings deposits increase in the North West region" "most preferred banking products in 2024" and so on. This way, they don't have to look through transaction reports, financial statements, and customer details. Copilots can also give you information about someone's creditworthiness, make business ideas, and flag activities that seem fishy.

Retail

Retailers are always trying to figure out what customers want, what makes them buy certain things, and how and why their tastes change. All of these questions are easy for stores to answer with copilots for data analytics. Retailers can learn more about trends and better serve their customers by asking copilots questions like "What are the best stores in 2024?" and "Which discount coupons were used the most in December 2023?" this helps them understand the needs of their customers and improve their service.

Customer Support

Copilots can show you what kinds of requests people are making, what questions they are asking a lot, and what problems they are having most of the time. These tips can help people who work in customer service solve problems faster, give better advice, and make sure customers are happier. Product development teams can get useful information and ideas from customer support data to make goods, the customer journey, and the general experience better.

Marketing

Marketing teams need to communicate with their customers in a way that gets results. When marketing leaders use copilot for data analytics, they can find the channels that get the most traffic, compare the leads that different social media platforms create, judge the success of campaigns, and keep track of their marketing budget and spending. It helps them understand not only what happened but also why and how it happened by reading recaps of key results. This gives them a full picture.

Human Resource Management

Copilots can help HR managers figure out what skills and training are needed, what the results of training are, and how well employees are doing. Simple questions like "Who are the best sales reps?" "What is the ratio of developers to testers in a project?" "What was the turnover rate in 2023?" "How many employees are proficient in Python?" and so on can help HR managers handle and improve their teams.

Benefits of using copilot for data analytics

Artificial intelligence (AI)--powered copilots for data analytics help people process and analyze data to find insights. According to a poll of business owners by Forbes Advisor in 2023, AI is seen as a benefit because it helps people make better decisions (44%), respond faster (53%), and avoid mistakes (48%).

Faster insights

Copilots make data analysis easier and help users quickly find root causes, get useful insights in real-time, see everything going on in a business, and easily do complicated analysis.

Improved data-driven decision-making

Decision-makers can better spot trends, patterns, and differences when they have personalized, easy-to-understand insight reports. This teaches people how to make decisions based on facts.

Ease of use

Copilots make it easy for business users to connect with company data, even if they don't know much about technology. They do this by using a conversational and natural interface.

Accelerated data processing

By using copilot, users can automate data cleaning and processing, make processes for preparing data better, boost efficiency, and cut down on the time it takes to get good quality data ready for analysis.

Improved productivity

Copilots give users the tools they need to do self-service analytics, which lets them act quickly and work efficiently, saving a lot of time and resources in the process of finding insights.

Improved data literacy

By getting rid of technical hurdles and making the insight searching process easier, copilots for data analytics give users the confidence to do their analysis. This boosts the uptake of analytics, raises data literacy, and promotes an organization-wide culture that is driven by data.

Investigating Copilot's Complete Range of Capabilities

To fully understand what Microsoft Copilot can do, you need to look into all of its features, functions, and possible uses. Additionally, Copilot can do many other things besides just writing code. Its main job is to provide clever code ideas and completions.

Here is an outline of all the things that Copilot can do:

1. **Code Completion and Suggestions:** Copilot gives smart ideas for how to finish writing code based on what is being written. It helps programmers write code faster by suggesting names for variables, functions, method calls, and other parts of code.
2. **Code Generation from Comments:** Copilot can make code snippets based on developer notes or natural language explanations. Developers can tell Copilot to write the necessary code by leaving a note that describes the desired feature in plain English.
3. **Code Refactoring Suggestions:** Copilot gives you code rewriting ideas, like how to make code run faster, read better, or follow best practices. It can find places in code that can be refactored and offer ways to make things better.
4. **Error Detection and Correction:** Copilot can help you find and fix mistakes in your code by suggesting different pieces of code or calling out grammar mistakes. It can look at the context of the code to find possible problems and give advice on how to fix them.
5. **Cross-Language Support:** Copilot works with many computer languages and can make smart ideas and complete code in many languages and frameworks. It can switch between

languages in a project without any problems and provide language-specific help when needed.

6. **Integration with Git Version Control:** Copilot works with Git version control without any problems, so developers can use Visual Studio Code to interact with their Git files. This integration lets you do things like commit changes, push and pull code, fix merge issues, and see the past of commits.

7. **Privacy and Security Controls:** Copilot protects your privacy, and developers can look at and change its privacy and security options as required. Copilot only stores and sends code fragments and user data within the local working environment. This protects the privacy and security of the data.

8. **Learning and Adaptation:** Copilot is always learning and changing based on how users connect with it and what they say. When developers use Copilot and add ideas to their code, it learns from these interactions and improves its models so that it can make better suggestions in the future.

9. **Natural Language Interaction:** Copilot can do more than just complete code. It can also understand natural language notes or descriptions that the creator gives it. Developers can use plain English to describe the features they need, and Copilot will quickly come up with code snippets that match what they say.

10. **Customization and Configuration:** Copilot lets you change how it works to fit your needs and the needs of your project. To get the most out of Copilot, developers can change settings for code ideas, privacy, security, and more.

By learning more about these features, developers can use Microsoft Copilot to get more done, write better code, and speed up the development process for a wide range of projects and tasks.

CHAPTER 5
USING COPILOT EFFECTIVELY

To get the most out of Microsoft Copilot, you need to use its features and functions to improve your writing and get more done.

Here are some useful tips for using Copilot:

1. **Understand Copilot's Capabilities:** Get to know Copilot's features and functions, such as code completion, code generation, error detection, and natural language interaction. Learning what Copilot can do will help you use it in the best way possible.
2. **Provide Clear Context:** When you write code or comments about functions, give Copilot a clear and concise context to help it understand what you mean. Copilot can make more accurate and useful ideas when the situation is clear.
3. **Review Suggestions Carefully:** Copilot makes smart suggestions, but you need to carefully read them over before adding them to your code. Make sure that the code snippets that were offered meet your needs, follow coding standards, and fit with the design of your project.
4. **Validate Generated Code:** If you use Copilot to make code from natural language statements, make sure the code you made works the way you want it to. Use your coding environment to test the code pieces and make any changes that are needed.
5. **Provide Feedback:** If Copilot gives you wrong or less-than-ideal ideas, please let it know so it can get better at doing its job. You can give feedback right in Visual Studio Code or through the feedback methods on GitHub.
6. **Customize Settings:** You can change Copilot's settings to make it work the way you want it to and meet the needs of your project. You can change settings for code ideas, privacy, security, and other things to get the most out of Copilot.
7. **Integrate with Git:** To speed up your development process, use Copilot's interface with Git version control. You can make changes, push and pull code, fix merge issues, and see the history of commits in Visual Studio Code by using Git commands.
8. **Stay Informed:** To find out about changes and improvements to Copilot, keep an eye on what Microsoft and GitHub say. To get the newest features and improvements, make sure you regularly update your Visual Studio Code and Copilot application.
9. **Learn Keyboard Shortcuts:** To get more done while coding, learn and use the keyboard tools that come with Copilot. Learn the tools that you can use to get to Copilot's features, ask for ideas, and accept completions.
10. **Practice and Experiment:** To get better at using Copilot, try it out in different code situations and get used to its features. The more you use Copilot, the better you'll understand what it can do and how to use those skills in your projects.

If you follow these tips, you'll be able to use Microsoft Copilot to improve the quality of your software projects, write code more quickly, and get more done.

Best Practices for Utilizing Copilot

To get the most out of Microsoft Copilot and keep the quality of your code high, you need to follow some best practices.

Here are some tips on how to use Copilot most effectively:

1. **Understand Copilot's Scope and Limitations:** Learn about what Copilot can do and what it can't do. Even though Copilot can be helpful, it's important to remember that it's not perfect and might not always give you the most suitable advice.
2. **Provide Clear Context:** When you use Copilot, give clear context by making comments and code that describe what you're doing. Copilot can better understand your goals and make better ideas if you describe them clearly and concisely.
3. **Review and Validate Suggestions:** Before adding Copilot's suggestions to your script, you should always carefully read through them. Check the created code to make sure it meets your needs, follows the rules for writing code, and fits with the design of your project.
4. **Be Selective with Suggestions:** Don't just go along with Copilot's suggestions without thinking about what they mean. Think carefully about which ideas to add to your code, taking things like readability, maintainability, and speed into account.
5. **Supervise Copilot's Output:** Copilot can make code snippets, but it's important to watch what it does and make any changes that are needed. Make sure that the code that is created works well with the code that you already have and doesn't add any mistakes or security holes.
6. **Use Copilot as a Learning Tool:** Don't use Copilot instead of learning how to code. Instead, use it to help you learn. You can try out new ways of writing code with Copilot, learn from its tips, and get a better grasp of basic computer ideas.
7. **Provide Feedback:** If Copilot gives you wrong or less-than-ideal ideas, please let it know so it can get better at doing its job. Copilot's models and algorithms are always getting better thanks to your input.
8. **Balance Automation with Manual Coding:** Use Copilot's automation features while also writing code by hand. Some coding jobs can be done faster with Copilot, but hand coding gives you more control and accuracy, especially in important or complicated situations.
9. **Maintain Code Consistency:** Make sure that your codebase uses the same writing style, naming standards, and design patterns. To keep the code easy to read and manage, Copilot's ideas should match your project's coding standards and conventions.
10. **Stay Informed about Updates:** To keep up with changes and improvements to Copilot, keep an eye on Microsoft and GitHub releases. Update your Copilot app often to get the newest features and bug fixes.

By using these best practices, you can get the most out of Microsoft Copilot to improve the quality of your code, speed up development processes, and make your writing more productive.

Improving Productivity with Copilot

AI (artificial intelligence) has been a part of our online lives for a long time, making personalized news reports, friend ideas, email autocomplete hints and other things. With Microsoft 365 Copilot, AI can now do everything it was meant to do. Copilot works with Word, Excel, PowerPoint, Outlook, Teams, and other popular Microsoft apps without any problems to give you real-time, personalized help. The amazing change from "AI on autopilot" to "AI as copilot" Copilot gives you safe, enterprise-level AI by combining the power of large language models (LLMs) with your business data. This makes it one of the most powerful efficiency tools in the world. Copilot brings a fresh, new way of working to the table that gives workers the freedom to improve their creativity, output, and skills while spending less time on boring tasks. CoPilot 365 makes everyday jobs more productive by using standard apps.

Here are three ways to use Microsoft 365 copilot:

- **Automated Data Analysis in Excel:** CoPilot 365 can do complicated data analysis jobs in Excel automatically. For example, it can quickly look at trends, do complex math, and make detailed reports, which saves hours of work that would have to be done manually.
- **Efficient Email Management in Outlook:** It helps you handle your emails by putting important ones at the top of the list, scheduling replies, and organizing your inbox so you spend less time sorting them.
- **Improved Document Creation in Word:** CoPilot 365 helps you make better documents by offering ways to improve the content, giving you formatting choices, and even writing text for you based on short instructions. This makes the process of making documents much faster.

Here are five ways that Copilot can help you get more done:

1. **Write, edit, and summarize text in Word**

To get the most out of Word, give Copilot short instructions on how to do things while you work. Copilot can make drafts of documents, summarize text, redo parts of documents, change their tone, and more.

Examples of commands:

- Make the document sound less formal.
- Reduce the length of the third paragraph.
- Use the information from [a document] and [a table] to write a two-page plan.

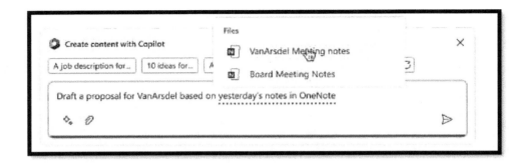

2. Unlock insights, identify trends, and generate powerful data visualizations in Excel

With Copilot in Excel, you can quickly look through and analyze your data. Copilot can help you make smart choices and meet your goals by giving you useful information, smart suggestions, and powerful visualizations.

Examples of commands:

- Show how the sales are broken down by type and channel. Put in a table.
- Make a chart to help you see what the effects of changing [a variable] will be.
- Figure out what would happen to my profit margin if the growth rate for [variable] changed.

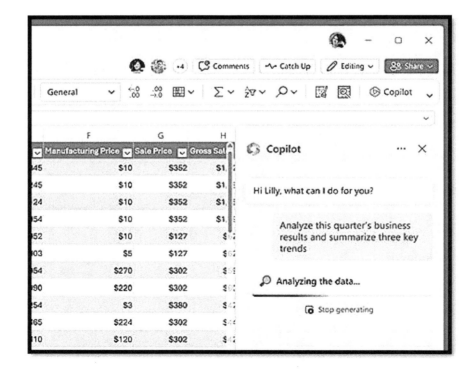

3. Accelerate the creation process and produce dynamic presentations in PowerPoint

You can use Copilot in PowerPoint to make amazing slideshows, change current slides, and add cool animations. Copilot can speed up your work and help you make high-quality shows that make the best use of all the features and tools that are available.

Examples of commands:

- Make a file slide show from [a paper] and add important stock photos.
- This talk should be summed up in three slides.
- Put these three bullet points in three boxes, and give each one a picture.

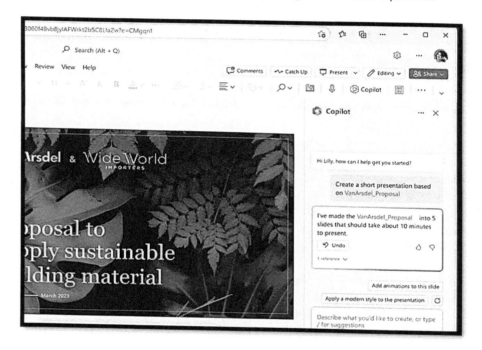

4. Manage your inbox and level up your communication in Outlook

With Copilot, you don't have to spend time going through texts and writing notes. Copilot in Outlook can sort emails, summarize long email lines, and write professional, high-quality notes. Copilot can add other emails or information from Microsoft 365 to your message.

Examples of commands:

- Write up a list of the emails I missed last week while I was away. Mark any important things.

3. **Explore New Coding Patterns:** You can use Copilot to find and try out new coding patterns, methods, and libraries. Try tackling coding jobs in different ways and follow Copilot's advice to improve your code knowledge and skills.
4. **Refactor Code Efficiently:** Copilot can help with code rewriting by suggesting ways to make code easier to read, run faster, or keep up to date. You can speed up the process of optimizing and restructuring your coding by using Copilot's refactoring ideas.
5. **Prototype Ideas Quickly:** When you're testing new features or ideas, you can use Copilot to make code scaffolds or sample versions based on what you say. Rapid code creation in Copilot can help you test and improve ideas more quickly.
6. **Learn from Copilot's Suggestions:** While you're writing, pay attention to what Copilot says. Look at the code snippets and patterns that Copilot suggests to learn new phrases, best practices, and ways to code.
7. **Collaborate with Teammates:** Share Copilot's ideas and code snippets with your teammates to make it easier for them to work together and share what they know. Copilot can help your team follow the same coding rules and make sure that the quality of the code is always the same.
8. **Optimize Documentation and Comments:** To make docs or comments for your script, use Copilot. Use normal language to explain how or why a piece of code works, and Copilot will create comments that go with it to make the code easier to read and manage.
9. **Stay Focused on High-Value Tasks:** Let Copilot do the regular coding tasks so you can focus on more important tasks, like designing the architecture, improving speed, or adding features. Let Copilot do the boring, repetitive writing work while you work on things that need you to think critically and creatively.
10. **Provide Feedback for Improvement:** Keep telling Microsoft and GitHub what you think about Copilot. Share your thoughts, ideas, and requests for new features to help make Copilot more accurate, useful, and easy to use over time.

These tips will help you get the most out of Microsoft Copilot to make your software development projects more productive, your writing process more efficient, and the quality of your work better.

Customizing Copilot Suggestions

By giving clear context, following coding standards, and changing the way you code, you can indirectly change the ideas.

Here are some good ways to change the ideas that Copilot makes:

1. **Clear Context:** To help Copilot understand your ideas better, make sure the context in your code and notes is clear and to the point. To help Copilot make the right choices, be very clear about the feature you're adding or the issue you're trying to fix.
2. **Coding Style and Conventions:** Make sure that your project uses the same coding style and rules throughout. Copilot learns from the patterns and styles in your files, so making

sure that your code is consistent helps it make ideas that are in line with the standards for your project.

3. **Feedback Mechanisms:** Tell Microsoft and GitHub what you think about Copilot's ideas, especially if you find tips that are wrong or not very good. Your feedback helps Copilot make its models and algorithms better, which makes ideas better over time.

4. **Code Reviews:** Have regular code reviews with your team to look over Copilot's ideas. As part of the review process, talk about the quality and usefulness of the code snippets that Copilot created and make any changes or fixes that are needed.

5. **Manual Intervention:** Even though Copilot makes ideas automatically, you are still in charge of choosing which code is added to your project. Carefully look over Copilot's ideas and make any necessary changes or improvements manually to make sure the code meets your needs and standards.

6. **Experimentation and Learning:** Try out the ideas that Copilot gives you and learn from the code snippets that it creates. Check out the different coding patterns, methods, and ways that Copilot suggests to get better at writing code and understanding how programming works.

7. **Selective Acceptance:** Be picky about which Copilot ideas you add to your software. Check each idea to see if it fits with the goals of your project, is relevant, and can be read and maintained. You should only accept ideas that make your software better and help your project.

8. **Continuous Improvement:** Always look for ways to make Copilot's ideas and the way you code better. To get better results over time, give Copilot feedback regularly, adjust to changes in how it acts, and improve the way you code.

Even though Copilot doesn't have as many customization options as some other tools, these tips can help you change Copilot's ideas to better fit the goals and preferences of your project.

CHAPTER 6

WORKING WITH COPILOT IN DIFFERENT SCENARIOS

1. **Automated Data Analysis**: Every week, a financial expert looks at market trends for hours. With Copilot, they can enter data and get a full report right away, which saves them hours of work.

2. **Improved Efficiency in Excel**: It used to take an HR manager a whole day to put together measures for employee success. This job can be done by Copilot in just a few hours, giving you more time to plan strategically.

3. **AI-Powered Insights**: Copilot is used by a marketing team to look at customer comments. It quickly shows them the most important opinion trends, which helps them make better strategic changes.

4. **Error Reduction**: An accountant who writes data by hand makes a lot of mistakes. These mistakes are less likely to happen with Copilot's formula ideas and data checking, which makes financial reports more reliable.

5. **Quick Formula Generation**: When a research worker is looking at large sets of complex data, they use Copilot to help them find relevant formulas. This speeds up the analysis process and cuts down on the time it takes to make formulas by hand.

6. **Time-Saving in Report Generation**: It used to take a project manager several hours to put together project progress reports, but now they use Copilot to quickly gather data and make full reports.

7. **Improved Decision-Making**: A sales manager looks at sales statistics from different areas using Copilot. The information given helps them better use their resources, which leads to more sales.

8. **Easy Data Visualization**: A school teacher who wants to see how students are doing across several different factors now uses Copilot to make maps. This makes it easier to see quickly which areas need more work.

9. **Interactive Data Exploration**: A store business analyst uses Copilot to look into sales data and interact with it to find secret trends and useful information.

10. **Enabled Workflows**: A transportation assistant manages inventory data with Copilot. It makes their job easier and makes it easier to keep track of stock and replace it.

11. **Personalized Data Handling**: A sales executive can change Copilot so that it only shows key success indicators that are important to their goals. This way, they can get customized reports that help them plan their strategy.

12. **Collaboration Improvement**: Copilot lets members of a cross-functional team doing market research work together to study and make sense of data. This improves teamwork and understanding.

13. **Learning Curve Reduction**: A non-profit with little technical know-how uses Copilot to make complicated Excel features easier to use so that staff can do advanced data jobs without having to go through a lot of training.

14. **Cost-Effectiveness**: A small business owner who doesn't have the money to buy expensive data analysis tools can process complex data with Copilot, which means they don't have to buy any more software.

15. **Real-Time Data Processing**: An operations manager uses Copilot to handle real-time inventory data, which lets them make decisions about transportation and restocking right away.

16. **Support for Complex Calculations**: An environmental scientist uses Copilot to do complicated statistical analysis that would need special statistical tools otherwise.

17. **Intuitive User Interface**: An independent writer who doesn't know much about Excel uses Copilot because it's easy to use and helps them organize and analyze research data quickly.

18. **Customizable Outputs**: A financial consulting company changes the outputs from Copilot to fit its reporting style. This makes it easier to make reports for clients.

19. **Data Integrity Maintenance**: An academic researcher uses Copilot to analyze data and makes sure that the security of their study data is kept up throughout the process.

20. **Flexible Data Manipulation**: In a transportation company, the supply chain manager uses Copilot to change package data in a variety of ways, which helps find the best routes and lowers the cost of shipping.

21. **Improved Data Interpretation**: A real estate company uses Copilot to make sense of complicated market data, which lets managers give their clients better tips on how to invest in real estate.

22. **Productivity Tracking**: An IT company uses Copilot to keep track of the progress of a project. This makes it easier to figure out how productive people are and how much work they have to do.

23. **Scalable Solutions**: An e-commerce company that is growing uses Copilot's scalable features to handle more sales data without having to spend a lot of money on more IT staff.

24. **Secure Data Handling**: A healthcare provider trusts Copilot to keep patient data safe and secure in meeting privacy and security standards.

25. **Integration with Microsoft Suite**: The fact that Copilot works with Microsoft Suite makes it easier for a law company to prepare documents and analyze data across multiple programs.

26. **Reduced Training Requirements**: A public school system uses Copilot, lowering teachers' need for thorough Excel training, thereby saving time and resources.

27. **Accessibility Features**: An NGO with staff members who aren't all tech-savvy uses Copilot and likes how its accessibility features make data analysis more open to everyone.

28. **Language Support**: Copilot's growing language support helps an international company's teams communicate and share data more easily around the world.

29. **Continuous Improvement**: The changes and improvements to Copilot help a tech company keep its data analysis tools on the cutting edge.

30. **Future-Proofing**: An investment company stays on top of technology by using Copilot to train its employees for new AI developments and changes in the industry.

Software Development

To make Copilot work well for you in software development, follow these steps:

1. **Installation**: First, add the GitHub Copilot app to Visual Studio Code. You can find "GitHub Copilot" in VS Code's store of addons and install it that way.
2. **Enable Copilot**: You may need to sign in with your GitHub account after downloading to turn on Copilot. As soon as you turn Copilot on, it starts making suggestions as you write code.
3. **Contextual Suggestions**: Copilot looks at the background of your code and makes ideas based on what it finds. The code you've already written can help it come up with variable names, function names, code completions, and even whole functions or blocks of code.
4. **Interactiveness**: You can talk to Copilot. As you type, it offers code completions. You can accept or reject these ideas by pressing the Tab key. You can also use the arrow keys to move between different ideas.
5. **Code Generation**: Python, JavaScript, TypeScript, Ruby, Go, Java, and other computer languages can all be used by Copilot to make code. It works especially well for jobs that need to be done over and over or for making basic code.
6. **Learning and Feedback**: The code you write and the changes you make help Copilot learn. It gets smarter over time and makes better ideas based on how you code and what you like.
7. **Code Review Assistance**: Copilot can help with code reviews by offering changes that would make the code better or by pointing out problems that might be in the code. This can help make sure that the code quality and accuracy are kept up across the whole project.
8. **Privacy and Security**: Be careful with the code you give Copilot, especially if it has private data in it. Copilot doesn't store your code, but it does learn from the pieces of code it sees. Be careful using Copilot with codebases that are private or owned by someone else.
9. **Feedback and Reporting**: If you use Copilot and run into any bugs or strange behavior, you can let GitHub know. Reporting problems and giving comments helps the tool get better over time.
10. **Continuous Learning**: Keep looking into what Copilot can do and what it suggests. Try out different kinds of writing to figure out when and how it can help your growth process the most.

You can be more productive, spend less time writing code manually, and maybe even find new coding patterns and best practices by using Copilot in your software development process. But it's important to use Copilot as a tool, not as an alternative for human reasoning and software development know-how.

Code Refactoring

Copilot can be a useful tool for rewriting code, which helps developers make codebases more efficient and better. Here are some good ways to use Copilot for changing code:

1. **Identify Refactoring Opportunities**: To begin, look through your coding and find places where rewriting could be useful. This could be code that is used more than once, methods or functions that are too long, conditional statements that are too complicated, algorithms that don't work well, or old ways of writing code.
2. **Review Suggestions**: As you look through your code, Copilot will give you rewriting ideas that make sense in that context. Some of these ideas are to remove methods, change the names of variables, make conditionals easier to understand, improve loops, and more.
3. **Evaluate Suggestions**: Look over Copilot's suggestions to see if they make sense and how they might affect your software. Think about things like readability, maintainability, speed, and following the code rules.
4. **Customize Suggestions**: Copilot's ideas aren't always right, so you may need to change them to fit your needs. You can change the suggested code to make it fit better with the way you code, the rules of the project, or the functionality needs.
5. **Apply Refactoring Techniques**: Here are some refactoring techniques that you can use with Copilot: method extraction, variable renaming, code reduction, loop optimization, and algorithm simplicity. Based on the chosen context, Copilot can make the code bits needed for this refactoring.
6. **Test Thoroughly**: After making changes to your code through rewriting, make sure you test it carefully to make sure that it still works the way it should. Automated tests can help you find a regression that were caused by rewriting and make sure that your software is stable generally.
7. **Document Changes**: Write down the refactoring changes you've made to your program to make it clearer and easier to manage. You can add notes, update documents, or write pull request descriptions to explain why the refactoring was done and how it will affect the software.
8. **Iterate and Improve**: Refactoring is an iterative process, and you may need to make changes more than once to get the quality and maintainability of the code you want. Keep an eye on the codebase all the time to find more chances to change it, and use Copilot to help you make small improvements over time.
9. **Review and Collaboration**: If you're working with other developers, have them help you review the code and give you feedback on the changes you made during rewriting. During code reviews, Copilot can help you come up with reasons or examples to back up your rewriting choices.
10. **Learn from Suggestions**: Use Copilot's ideas to learn new ways to refactor code, improve your writing, and follow best practices. You can learn more about software design concepts and get better at writing code over time by looking at the suggested refactoring.

Overall, Copilot can be a helpful tool for refactoring code. It can make the process easier and better the quality of your coding by making smart ideas and automating tasks. However, it's important to use Copilot as a tool to help you learn more about software development and not just rely on its ideas.

Code Review

Even though Copilot can be very helpful for code review, here are some things to think about and best practices to follow:

1. **Understanding of Context**: Copilot writes code based on what the current coding and notes say about the situation. It is very important to make sure that Copilot fully comprehends the project's needs and limitations. Copilot can make better ideas if you give clear, concise feedback and background information during code reviews.
2. **Code Quality and Best Practices**: Copilot can quickly come up with code, but it's important to check the quality of the code it offers. Make sure that the code that is created follows best practices, follows writing standards, and stays the same as the codebase that is already there. Reviewers should check to see if the suggested code is easy to read, works well, and can be maintained.
3. **Security and Compliance**: Copilot might not know about the exact compliance or security rules that apply to your project. Reviewers should pay close attention to any possible security holes or compliance problems in the suggested code and make sure that the right steps are taken to fix them.
4. **Integration with Existing Processes**: Copilot can be easily added to the code review process you already have in place. Make it clear when and how to use Copilot during code review, and make sure everyone on the team knows what these rules are. To properly analyze the ideas made by Copilot, encourage team members to work together and talk about them.
5. **Human Oversight and Judgment**: Even though Copilot can write code automatically, it's important to remember that code review still needs human oversight and judgment. Reviewers should think carefully about the ideas that Copilot makes, taking into account things like whether the logic is correct, how well the program works, and any edge cases that the AI might not have thought of.
6. **Feedback and Improvement**: Tell Copilot what you think by approving or refusing its ideas and explaining why you made the choices you did. This feedback helps Copilot learn and get better over time, which means that in the future when it reviews code, it will make ideas that are more accurate and useful.

By adding Microsoft Copilot to your code review process smartly and responsibly, you can use its features to boost productivity and code quality while keeping your team in charge of the development process.

Pair Programming

Pair programming with Microsoft Copilot can be a great experience, but there are a few things you should keep in mind to get the most out of it:

1. **Establish Clear Roles**: Figure out what each pair programmer's job is. One person can focus on driving (writing code), while the other person watches and thinks about what Copilot says. Change jobs every so often to make sure that both developers are involved and making good contributions.
2. **Use Copilot as a Collaborative Tool**: Think of Copilot as an extra team member, not as a substitute for human developers. Talk about the ideas that Copilot makes with each other, decide if they are useful, and then decide if they should be added to the script.
3. **Leverage Copilot's Strengths**: Based on the information you give it, Copilot can quickly create code snippets. To get more done during pair programming sessions, use its ability to offer different solutions, suggest improvements, and handle repetitive jobs.
4. **Maintain Communication**: It's very important to be able to talk to each other clearly when you are pair programming, especially when you're using Copilot. Talk about why Copilot made the choices it did, clear up any confusion, and make sure everyone is on the same page about the code that is being written.
5. **Balance Autonomy and Control**: Copilot can give you good ideas, but you still need to be in charge of the software. When deciding whether to accept or refuse Copilot's ideas, use your judgment and think about things like the quality of the code, how easy it is to keep, and how well it fits the project's needs.
6. **Educate and Learn**: Use your time working together on computer projects with Copilot as a chance to learn new things and improve your skills. Talk about your ideas, share your writing skills, and learn from each other's mistakes to get better as developers.
7. **Provide Feedback to Copilot**: Based on the ideas it makes during pair programming meetings, give Copilot feedback. By letting Copilot know whether you agree with its ideas or not and giving reasons for your choices, you help it learn and get better over time.

Overall, adding Microsoft Copilot to pair programming can improve teamwork, output, and code quality if it is used correctly with human developers when working together. Pairs can use Copilot to speed up their development process and get high-quality code out quickly by playing to its strengths and keeping communication and control open and clear.

CHAPTER 7

COPILOT AND OPEN-SOURCE COLLABORATION

By giving developers AI-generated ideas and code snippets, Microsoft Copilot can have a big effect on how people work together on open-source projects.

Here's how Copilot can make working together on open-source projects better:

1. **Increased Productivity**: Copilot can offer code snippets, libraries, and solutions, so developers don't have to do the same things over and over again. This can speed up the growth process in open-source projects, giving users more time to work on bigger issues and new ideas.
2. **Accessibility and Inclusivity**: Copilot can help workers of all skill levels, even those who are new to open-source projects. Helpful ideas and instructions make open-source teamwork easier to access and open to a wider range of developers. This makes coding more democratic.
3. **Accessibility and Inclusivity**: By offering best practices, following coding standards, and avoiding common mistakes, Copilot can help keep code quality and consistency high across open-source projects. This can make the codebase more reliable and easier to manage, which is good for both authors and users.
4. **Learning and Skill Development**: Copilot helps developers learn about code methods, algorithms, and the best ways to do things. Contributors can improve their skills and knowledge by looking into Copilot's ideas and understanding why it makes the choices it does. This encourages ongoing learning in the open-source community.
5. **Collaborative Problem Solving**: Copilot encourages open-source participants to work together to solve problems by coming up with different ideas and setting up conversations about how to execute code. Developers can use Copilot's ideas as starting places for working together, trying out different methods, and improving solutions as a group.
6. **Feedback and Improvement**: Working together with Copilot in an open-source way lets you give feedback to the AI model, which helps it learn and get better over time. People can add to Copilot's training data by either taking or rejecting its ideas. This gives the company useful information that can help future users make it more accurate and useful.
7. **Enhanced Documentation and Examples**: Copilot can help make open-source projects' instructions and examples easier to read and understand for users and participants. Copilot helps improve the documentation of open-source projects by offering code comments, descriptions, and usage examples.

Overall, Microsoft Copilot could change the way people work together on open-source projects by giving workers AI-generated help, which would increase productivity, quality, community participation, and learning within the open-source community. Open-source projects can speed up development, improve code quality, and involve a wide range of users by using Copilot as a joint tool.

Leveraging Copilot in Open-Source Projects

Microsoft Copilot is a powerful AI-powered tool that helps developers write code by suggesting changes and finishing lines as they go. When used in open-source projects, Copilot can boost output and make development go more smoothly.

Here are some good ways to use Copilot in your open-source projects:

1. **Integrating Copilot into Development Workflow**: Make sure that Copilot works well with your development setup. Microsoft makes plugins for popular code editors like Visual Studio Code that make it easy for developers to use Copilot's ideas and completions while they code.
2. **Understanding Copilot's Capabilities**: Start by learning about what Copilot can do and what it can't do. Copilot can come up with code snippets based on the information you give it, but it's important to check the ideas carefully to make sure they meet the project's needs and writing standards.
3. **Collaborative Development**: Use Copilot to help participants understand the codebase and make ideas during code reviews to encourage teamwork in the open-source community. Copilot can speed up the code review process by finding mistakes and offering ways to make things better.
4. **Augmenting Documentation**: For instructions, tutorials, and README files, use Copilot to make code samples. This can make it easier for new people to join the project and show them how to use different parts of it.
5. **Increasing Productivity**: Copilot can make you much more productive by handling jobs that you do over and over again, like writing boilerplate code, utility functions, or common design patterns. Developers don't have to spend as much time on boring coding jobs and can instead focus on fixing hard problems.
6. **Ensuring License Compliance**: If you use Copilot in an open-source project, make sure that the code it creates follows the license rules of that project. It's important to check that the code can be used within the project's licensing system because Copilot may offer code snippets that come from different sources.
7. **Providing Feedback to Improve Copilot**: As you use Copilot in your open-source projects, let Microsoft know what you think about it so they can make it more accurate and useful. You can help improve Copilot's features by reporting problems, making improvements, and sharing your own experiences.
8. **Respecting Copyright and Intellectual Property**: Even though Copilot helps you write code, it's important to keep intellectual property and copyright rights in mind. Do not use Copilot to make code that directly copies or violates intellectual property rights, private formulas, or patented methods.

Developers can improve teamwork, speed, and code quality in open-source projects by using Microsoft Copilot. They can also help AI-assisted development tools get better. But it's important to use Copilot properly, follow the rules for licensing, and code honestly.

Maintaining Code Quality and Licensing Compliance

To keep the codebase's identity and follow the law, it's important to keep up with code quality and licensing issues when using Microsoft Copilot in open-source projects. **Here are some ways to make this happen:**

1. **Review Generated Code**: Copilot can give you good code ideas, but it's still important to carefully read the code that it made. Check to see if the code follows coding standards, works with other code, and can be improved. Make sure the code is well-documented and follows the right way to do things.

2. **Manual Verification**: Don't rely on code written by Copilot alone; check it by hand too. Check that the code follows the project's goals, design, and rules for writing code. Check that the created code works as expected and that it doesn't pose any security risks.

3. **Licensing Awareness**: When you use Copilot, keep in mind that it might affect your license. Make sure that the code that is created follows the license that was picked for the project. If Copilot offers code fragments from outside sources, make sure they meet the licensing needs of the project.

4. **Attribution**: If Copilot offers code snippets from outside sources that need to be credited, make sure that the right credit is given in the project's instructions or source files. Respect the intellectual property rights of people who contribute code and tools that are not your own.

5. **Legal Review**: If you're not sure about license or copyright problems with code made by Copilot, you should talk to a lawyer to make sure you're following all the laws and rules that apply. Legal professionals can help you get licenses in tricky situations and lower your legal risks.

6. **Educate Contributors**: Teach project members how to use Copilot and how important it is to keep the quality of the code high and make sure that the license is followed. They should be told to look over and confirm the code written by Copilot before adding it to the main file. Give contributors rules and tools to help them make smart choices.

7. **Regular Audits**: Check the source regularly to find and fix any problems with quality or not following the rules. Use both automatic and human methods to look for possible license violations, duplicate codes, and other quality issues.

8. **Community Engagement**: Create a clear and open development space where people can talk about and solve problems with code made by Copilot. Open up lines of contact and ask for comments to keep improving the quality of code and compliance practices.

These tips will help open-source projects use Microsoft Copilot effectively while keeping code quality high and following license rules. It's important to find a mix between using Copilot to get more done and making sure the code that comes out of it meets law and quality standards.

Community Guidelines and Etiquette

Setting clear community rules and etiquette is important for creating a polite and collaborative atmosphere when using Microsoft Copilot in open-source projects. **Here are some important things to think about:**

1. **Respect Intellectual Property Rights**: Stress how important it is to protect intellectual property rights when using Copilot. Get people who want to help write their code or use open-source tools with licenses that work with yours. Do not use Copilot to make code that breaks patents, copyrights, or other forms of intellectual property.

2. **Attribution and Licensing**: Remind authors that code snippets created by Copilot need to be properly attributed, especially if they come from outside sources or their licenses say they need to be. Make sure that the license rules for the project are understood and followed.

3. **Quality over Quantity**: Put quality code ahead of number code. Ask contributors to look over and confirm Copilot-generated code to make sure it fits the project's standards for being easy to read, update, and run quickly. Don't let people use Copilot without first thinking about whether it's right for them and what it means.

4. **Transparent Communication**: Encourage open and honest contact in the community. Encourage members to talk about how they openly use Copilot, share their stories, and ask other people for feedback. Set up places in the community, like email lists or boards, where people can ask questions, share ideas, and talk about problems they're having with using Copilot.

5. **Collaborative Decision-Making**: Get the community involved in how Copilot is used in decision-making processes. Ask participants for their thoughts on the rules, best practices, and guidelines that will control how Copilot is used in the project. Encourage a sense of belonging and acceptance by listening to different points of view and meeting different tastes.

6. **Educational Resources**: Give people in the community educational tools and training materials to help them use Copilot well. Give developers training, documents, and classes to help them learn about Copilot's features, limits, and ethical issues. Give participants the information they need to make smart choices and use Copilot wisely.

7. **Code Review Practices**: Set up code review practices that include carefully looking over code that was made by Copilot. Encourage thorough reviews to find possible problems, make the code better, and make sure it follows the rules and guidelines of the group. Give participants comments to help them get better at using Copilot and writing code.

8. **Code of Conduct**: Make sure everyone follows a set of rules that encourages acceptance, variety, and respect for each other in the group. Don't let discrimination, abuse, or other bad behavior happen. Make sure that all conversations about using Copilot follow the project's code of behavior and are done properly.

Setting clear rules and manners for using Microsoft Copilot in the community can help open-source projects create a helpful and positive space.

CHAPTER 8

ETHICAL CONSIDERATIONS AND CHALLENGES

There are big benefits to Microsoft Copilot in terms of speed and code quality, but it also brings up some social issues that need to be carefully dealt with.

Let's look into these points:

Ethical Considerations

1. **Data Privacy and Security**: Copilot learns from a huge number of code sources that are open to the public. But it is very important to make sure that this info is used honestly and safely. If Copilot offers code bits that look too much like protected work, you might accidentally reveal private or secret information or code.
2. **Intellectual Property Concerns**: Copilot writes code based on trends it learns from different sources. There is a chance that it will make code that violates patents or copyrights without meaning to. Microsoft needs to make sure that Copilot doesn't help people write code that steals other people's ideas.
3. **Bias and Fairness**: When it comes to bias and fairness, the datasets that Copilot learns from might have flaws that are common in the code community. These prejudices might show up as race, gender, or socioeconomic prejudices. To make sure that code ideas are fair and equal, Microsoft needs to take steps to find and fix these flaws.
4. **Accountability and Transparency**: It's important to set up ways for people to be held accountable for following Copilot's advice. Even if AI helps them, developers should know that they are ultimately responsible for the code they write. Microsoft should also be clear about what data Copilot learns from and how it comes up with ideas.
5. **Impact on Employment**: Some people are worried that tools like Copilot could replace human workers or make some code jobs less popular. Even though it can increase output, it's important to think about the bigger social and economic effects, such as job loss and the need to learn new skills.

Challenges

1. **Legal Complexity**: It can be hard to figure out the laws that govern code creation and intellectual property. Legal experts need to work closely with Microsoft to make sure that Copilot follows copyright laws and doesn't make it easier for people to steal other people's code.
2. **Quality Control**: It is very important to make sure that the code that Copilot writes is right and of high quality. Even though it's meant to help developers, giving them wrong or broken advice could leave software open to attacks or damage its security. To lower this risk, it is very important to set up strong quality control systems.
3. **Algorithmic Transparency**: Because machine learning methods are so complicated, it can be hard to understand how Copilot comes up with code ideas. To build trust and make it easier to fix problems when they happen, Microsoft needs to let developers know how Copilot makes decisions.
4. **Mitigating Biases**: It's hard to get rid of biases in Copilot's training data and algorithms. To make sure that code ideas aren't biased, Microsoft needs to use methods like data preprocessing, algorithmic fairness checks, and diverse dataset curation.
5. **User Education and Awareness**: Developers need to know what Copilot can and can't do so they can use it safely and successfully. Microsoft should put money into broad user

education and knowledge programs to encourage developers to make smart choices and encourage developers to use technology ethically.

Addressing Bias and Fairness Concerns

It is important to fix problems with bias and fairness in technologies like Microsoft Copilot to make sure that software development is fair and includes everyone. As artificial intelligence (AI) becomes more commonplace in our daily lives, it's important to deal with flaws that might keep discrimination or unfairness going.

In this case, Microsoft Copilot, a tool meant to help developers finish and generate code, needs to be checked for any possible flaws and fairness problems, and steps need to be taken to fix them.

1. **Understanding Bias in AI**: Many things can cause bias in AI systems, such as biased training data, biased algorithms, or biased encounters with users. Copilot might show bias in the code ideas it makes, the computer languages it supports, or the code examples it picks out as most useful.
2. **Diverse Representation in Training Data**: To avoid bias, Copilot needs to be taught on datasets that are both varied and representative. To do this, the training data needs to include a lot of different computer languages, styles of writing, and types of problems. Also, developers from a variety of backgrounds should be encouraged to contribute so that the project doesn't favor certain groups of people or points of view by accident.
3. **Algorithmic Fairness**: The formulas that run Microsoft Copilot must be made fairly. To do this, detailed audits must be done to find and fix biases at both the personal and systemic levels. Fairness-aware learning and algorithmic openness are two techniques that can help reduce bias and make sure that everyone gets the same results.
4. **Bias Detection and Mitigation Tools**: Microsoft should build strong tools for finding and fixing biases in Copilot's ideas. This could mean adding tools that look for patterns of bias in the code that is created and marking possibly problematic areas so that developers can look them over. Adding the option for users to give comments on the tool's ideas can also help find and fix biases simultaneously.
5. **Ethical Guidelines and Standards**: Microsoft should make sure that the creation and use of Copilot are done in a way that follows clear ethical rules and guidelines. Fairness, openness, and responsibility should be at the top of these rules, and they should be followed throughout the lifecycle of a product. Regular checks and reviews should also be done to make sure these standards are being followed and to find places where things could be better.
6. **User Education and Awareness**: To encourage responsible use, users must be taught about the possible flaws in AI systems like Copilot. Microsoft should give developers training and teaching materials on how to spot and fix bias in their code, as well as how to think critically about Copilot's ideas for making things fairer and more welcoming.

7. **Community Engagement and Collaboration**: To keep making Copilot fairer and more welcoming, it's important to keep working with the developer community to get feedback and new ideas. Microsoft should encourage open communication with users, researchers, and support groups to get feedback, solve concerns, and work together on ways to make the tool fairer.

8. **Transparency and Accountability**: Microsoft needs to put openness and accountability at the top of its list of priorities when making and using Copilot. This means making sure there is clear information about how the tool works, how it deals with bias, and how users can report problems or give comments. The company should also be open about how it makes decisions and take responsibility for fixing any problems with bias or fairness that come up.

To sum up, fixing problems with bias and unfairness in Microsoft Copilot requires a multifaceted approach that includes using training data from a variety of backgrounds, making sure the algorithm is fair, using tools to find and fix bias, teaching users about ethics, getting the community involved, being open and responsible, and being transparent. By putting these things at the top of their list of priorities, Microsoft can work to make the Copilot development setting fairer and more open to everyone.

Understanding the Limitations of Copilot

Microsoft Copilot is a code completion tool driven by AI that was made by OpenAI and GitHub. The goal of Copilot is to help developers by giving them code ideas based on the details of their projects using OpenAI's GPT (Generative Pre-trained Transformer) models. Copilot has gotten a lot of attention because it could make developers more productive, but it's important to know what it can't do before adding it to your software development process.

1. **Contextual Understanding Limitations:**

Domain Specificity: The training data that Copilot has seen is a big part of how well it can make code ideas. Copilot's ideas might not be right or useful if the software or project is very specific or if it uses frameworks or languages that aren't well covered in the training data.

Handling Ambiguity: Copilot may have trouble understanding standards that aren't clear or aren't stated well. In this case, it might make code fragments that don't fully match the developer's needs or plans.

2. **Security and Privacy Concerns:**

Data Privacy: A lot of the code that makes Copilot work is available on GitHub, which makes people worry about the privacy of private or secret code bits. Even though GitHub has taken steps to protect sensitive code, developers should still be careful not to reveal private information by accident.

Security Vulnerabilities: Copilot might suggest pieces of code that have security holes by accident. Developers need to be careful and look over Copilot's ideas to make sure they follow best practices for security.

3. Overreliance on Copilot:

Code Ownership and Understanding: If developers rely too much on Copilot, it could hurt their ability to own and understand the software. If you rely too much on automatic code ideas without understanding how they work, you might end up with code that is hard to manage or fix.

Limited Learning Opportunities: If developers only use Copilot to generate code, they might miss out on important chances to learn. Actively working with the code and fixing problems on your own helps you understand it better and get better at it.

4. License and Intellectual Property Issues:

License Compliance: Copilot may suggest pieces of code that break software licenses by accident, especially when working with open-source projects that have strict licensing rules. Developers need to look over Copilot's ideas to make sure they follow the licenses that apply.

Intellectual Property Concerns: Copilot's ideas might violate intellectual property rights without meaning to, especially when creating code that looks like secret formulas or trademarked methods. Developers need to be careful to stay out of trouble with the law.

5. Bias and Ethical Concerns:

Bias in Code Suggestions: Copilot's training data may have flaws that are common in the software development community as a whole. This could show up as skewed code ideas for variable names, notes, or ways to run an algorithm. Being aware of these biases is important for lessening their effects.

Ethical Use of AI: When developers use AI-powered tools like Copilot, they need to think about the ethical problems that come up, such as fairness, responsibility, and openness. To make sure AI is used responsibly, it needs to be constantly checked for flaws and ethics issues and ways to deal with them.

6. Limitations in Handling Complex Logic:

Complex Problem Solving: Copilot might have trouble writing code for difficult computer jobs that need careful problem-solving or algorithmic optimization. When this happens, developers might have to use direct assistance or other methods to fix the problem.

Performance Optimization: When it comes to jobs that require a lot of computing power, Copilot's ideas may put clarity and simplicity ahead of performance optimization. For the best results, developers may need to tweak the code that is created.

7. Language and Documentation Limitations:

Support for Programming Languages: Copilot works with many computer languages, but it might not work as well with some languages or systems as with others. Copilot may not be able to generate all the code that developers need when they are using less popular languages or niche systems.

Documentation and Comments: Copilot's ideas might not have enough comments or documentation, which makes it hard for developers to understand why some code snippets are used. Manual notes and comments may be needed to make code easier to read and keep up to date. It is important to know what Microsoft Copilot can't do so that you can make the most of its features while minimizing risks and problems. By being aware of these limits and using the right methods to incorporate Copilot into the development process, developers can make the most of its potential to boost productivity and code quality while also making sure that AI is used responsibly and ethically. To get the most out of Copilot while also working around its flaws, it's important to evaluate, get comments on, and keep making it better.

Legal and Intellectual Property Implications

As an AI-powered code completion tool made by OpenAI and GitHub, Microsoft Copilot has a lot of law and intellectual property issues for both users and the companies involved.

Some important things to think about are:
  1. **License Compliance:**

Open Source Licenses: Copilot offers code based on how it has learned to use the huge amount of open-source code on GitHub. It is up to the developers to make sure that Copilot's code follows the rules set by the open-source projects it has learned from. Legal problems could happen if you don't follow these agreements.

Proprietary Code: When developers use Copilot with secret code, they need to be careful. It's important to read Copilot's advice so that you don't accidentally reveal or break trade secrets or private codes.

  2. **Intellectual Property (IP) Concerns:**

Potential Infringement: Copilot could make code that violates patents, copyrights, or other intellectual property rights without meaning to. To make sure that the code created by Copilot doesn't break third-party IP rights, developers need to be careful and do a lot of checks.

Algorithmic Similarity: Copilot's ideas may look a lot like copyrighted algorithms or secret methods. Developers should be aware of the chance of accidentally infringing on someone else's rights and take the right steps to lower this risk.

  3. **Data Privacy:**

Privacy of Code Snippets: Copilot's features depend on getting code snippets from GitHub sources that are open to the public. GitHub has taken steps to protect sensitive code, but developers should still be aware of how this might affect their privacy, especially when working with private or protected code.

  4. **Responsibility and Accountability:**

Attribution and Ownership: Developers should think about attribution and ownership problems when they use code created by Copilot. It is very important to give thanks to the original developers of the code and say where it came from.

Accountability for Code Quality: Copilot can help developers write code, but the developers are ultimately responsible for making sure the code is right and of good quality. The code that Copilot generates should be carefully looked over and tested by developers to make sure it meets their needs and standards.

  5. **Fair Use and Fair Dealing:**

Fair Use Considerations: Some of Copilot's ideas may include copyrighted information. When developers use copyrighted information, they need to make sure that they follow the rules about fair use or fair dealing. This means taking things like the reason and type of use, the amount of material used, and how it might affect the market for the original work into account.

  6. **End-User License Agreements (EULAs):**

Terms of Service: Developers who use Copilot should carefully read the Microsoft and GitHub terms of service and end-user license agreements (EULAs). There may be important parts of these deals about how to use Copilot, like warranties, intellectual property rights, and responsibility limits.

7. **Ethical Considerations:**

Bias and Representation: The training data for Copilot may have flaws that are common in the software development community as a whole. Developers should be aware of how these biases might affect the code that Copilot generates and take steps to reduce bias and make their software projects more diverse and welcoming.

As a conclusion, Microsoft Copilot can help developers write code, but it's important to think about the law and intellectual property issues that come up when they use it. Developers should be careful, follow all laws and rules, and do what they need to do to deal with possible risks and social issues. Also, developers, lawyers, and AI researchers working together can help figure out these tricky problems and make sure that AI-powered tools like Copilot are used responsibly and decently.

CHAPTER 9

FUTURE DEVELOPMENTS AND ROADMAP

The plans for Microsoft 365 Copilot are big. Along with Word, Excel, PowerPoint, Outlook, and Teams, it is built into several work tools. Plus, there are plans to add more features that will let it work with Microsoft's more advanced tools, such as Dynamics 365. Not only is Microsoft 365 Copilot a tool, but it's also a picture of how work will be done in the future. It promises to not only change how productive each person is but also how organizations work together and share information. As Microsoft continues to learn and come up with new ideas, one thing is clear: AI will power the bright future of work.

We fully back that future, and we think Martello is perfectly set up to support it too.

1. **Enhanced Language Support**: Microsoft Copilot may add support for more languages than just a few computer languages. It mostly worked with Go, Python, JavaScript, TypeScript, and Ruby. It would be more flexible and useful for a wider range of developers if it could handle more languages.
2. **Improved Code Understanding**: Copilot could get better at figuring out what the code means and how it works. This could mean getting better at dealing with patterns that are specific to a project, learning jargon that is specific to a field, and changing to different ways of writing code.
3. **Integration with Development Environments**: Visual Studio Code, JetBrains IDEs, and GitHub's online editor are just a few of the famous development environments that Microsoft Copilot could work better with. It would be easier for developers to use Copilot's ideas in their work if they were better integrated.
4. **Customization and Personalization**: It would be helpful to have choices for modification and personalization. Developers may want to change how Copilot works based on how they like to code, the needs of the project, or the standards of their team. This could mean setting writing standards, favorite tools, or even your code snippets.
5. **Security and Privacy Enhancements**: Because of worries about AI-generated code and possible security holes, Microsoft Copilot may spend money to make security features better. This could mean making sure that user privacy and data are protected and finding and fixing security holes in created code more quickly.
6. **Training with Feedback Loop**: One suggestion for the road map is to keep improving the AI model by using comments from developers. This feedback process would help Copilot figure out what went wrong and make its ideas better over time.
7. **Support for New Development Paradigms**: As ways of building software change, Copilot may change to support new ways of building software, like low-code development, serverless systems, or building machine learning models. To do this, you would need to understand these new concepts and write code pieces that work with them.

8. **Enterprise Features**: Microsoft Copilot could add features for business users that are designed to meet the needs of big software development teams. This could include better tools for working together, connecting to central repositories for business code, or helping with meeting legal requirements.

9. **Documentation and Learning Resources**: To help developers get the most out of Microsoft Copilot, it would be very helpful to have detailed literature, tutorials, and learning tools. This could include debugging tips, best practices for using Copilot in the development process, and examples of how to use the tool.

10. **Community Engagement and Open-Source Collaboration**: Microsoft Copilot could have a lively group of workers who work on it together, share tips and tricks, and make add-ons or plugins. Opening up some parts of Copilot to the public could also encourage developers to work together and come up with new ideas.

Microsoft Copilot's Role in Future Collaborations

As Microsoft Copilot keeps getting better, it will have a bigger effect on places where people work together. In later versions of Copilot, the following could be added:

1. **Real-time Collaboration Analytics**: By looking at how people work together, Copilot could give you information about how the team works and help you figure out what works well and what needs work. This could lead to better ways for teams to work together and be put together.

2. **Seamless Cross-Platform Integration**: Copilot will work better with more Microsoft tools and add-ons from other companies. With this addition, Copilot's insights and automation features will be able to be used in all team processes, no matter what platform is being used.

3. **Predictive Project Assistance**: Over time, Copilot could grow to not only help with current projects but also guess what projects will be needed in the future by offering ideas based on market trends, team strengths, and past wins.

4. **Emerging Functionalities**: Copilot could add new technologies like augmented reality for virtual meetings or blockchain for safe document sharing, which could expand the ways that teams can work together.

5. **Analysis and Commentary**: The way Microsoft Copilot and other similar AI tools are going points to a future where AI is an important and effective part of working together. These improvements should make things run more smoothly and help people come up with new ways to work together, which will lead to more creativity and innovation. But as these tools become more commonplace, it will be important to make sure they don't substitute for real interaction when people work together. To get the most out of AI in collaborative settings, it will be important to find a balance between new technology and keeping team spirit and imagination alive.

Potential Enhancements and Features

Of course! As an AI-powered code assistant, Microsoft Copilot has a huge amount of room for improvements and new features. Here are a few possible ways to make it better:

1. **Advanced Contextual Understanding**: Make it easier for Copilot to understand what the code being written is about. To give more accurate and useful code ideas could mean getting a better grasp on variable scopes, function contexts, and the general structure of the project.

2. **Code Quality Improvement Suggestions**: Add features that can give advice not only for finishing code but also for making it better. This could include suggestions for changing code, making it run faster, or following best practices and coding standards.

3. **Code Review Assistance**: Allow Copilot to help with code reviews by automatically finding possible problems, offering changes, or giving answers for certain code constructs. This could make the code review process go more quickly and help all development teams write better code.

4. **Customization and Preferences**: Users should be able to change how Copilot works based on how they code, their interests, and the needs of the project. This could include settings for writing standards, recommended libraries, rules for formatting code, and more.

5. **Integration with Version Control Systems**: Make it easier to use version control systems like Git so that the project's update history, branches, and merge requests can be used to make smarter ideas. This might help Copilot understand how the software has changed over time and make better ideas.

6. **Multi-Language Support**: Add more computer languages and tools to Copilot's language support list. This would make it a more useful tool for developers working on a range of projects using a range of technology stacks.

7. **Interactive Learning and Feedback Loop**: Make sure that Copilot can learn from real-time encounters and comments from users. This could mean using user feedback like corrections, scores, and notes to make the ideas better and more relevant over time.

8. **Code Generation Templates**: Give examples or templates for popular coding jobs, design patterns, or project structures with code generation templates. Making basic code that developers can then change to fit their needs, could help speed up development.

9. **Code Search and Documentation Integration**: Allow Copilot to look for code snippets and documentation from government literature, community forums, or code repositories, among other places. This would give developers more information and tools to use while they write code.

10. **Privacy and Security Controls**: Make sure that private data and proprietary code are not shared or revealed by accident by putting in place strong privacy and security controls. This could include giving users the chance to say what data privacy rules they need to follow and limiting code ideas.

11. **Support for Domain-Specific Languages**: Make Copilot work with domain-specific languages and frameworks that are popular in fields like banking, healthcare, and

scientific computers. This would meet the needs of developers who work in certain fields or businesses.

12. **Real-Time Collaboration Features**: Add features that will let multiple workers working with Copilot work together in real-time, sharing code snippets, writing code together, and giving each other feedback in the development environment.

With these possible additions and improvements, Microsoft Copilot could become an even more useful tool for workers in a wide range of fields and businesses.

Community Feedback and Contributions

Tools like Microsoft Copilot change and get better with the help of community comments and input. This is how Copilot could gain from getting involved in the community:

1. **Bug Identification and Reporting**: People in the community can help find bugs, glitches, or edge cases that weren't found during internal testing. They can report these problems, which gives the development team useful information to use to fix them.
2. **Feature Requests and Prioritization**: Users have different wants, processes, and ways of using the app. By asking the community for feature requests, the Copilot team can find out which improvements users would value the most and then focus their development efforts on those.
3. **Usability Testing**: Members of the community can help test Copilot's usefulness by giving comments on its user design, user experience, and general usability. You can use this input to find places where things could be easier to use, clearer, and more natural.
4. **Code Contributions**: Skilled developers in the community can help the Copilot project by adding new features, improving existing code, or making it run faster. This could mean sending in pull requests, making changes to open-source files, or even making add-ons and extensions for Copilot that make it work better.
5. **Documentation and Tutorials**: Members of the community can help make the documentation better, take lessons, and share the best ways to use Copilot. This can make it easier to get new users up and running and give current users more power to use Copilot to its fullest.
6. **Localization and Language Support**: The community can help translate Copilot into other languages, which makes it easier for developers all over the world to use. This could mean translating instructions, error messages, and user screens into different languages.
7. **Community Forums and Support**: Setting up community forums, discussion groups, or online communities just for Copilot can help users work together, share information, and help each other. People in the community can answer questions, help fix problems, and share useful information about how to use Copilot better.
8. **Feedback Loops and Iterative Development**: The Copilot team can set up feedback loops that allow for constant growth and iteration by interacting with the community. Over time, Copilot can be made better by regularly asking for feedback, looking at trends of use, and incorporating user ideas.

9. **Ethical Considerations and Guidelines**: Getting involved in the community can also help make sure that Copilot follows ethics rules and best practices. Decisions about data protection, artificial bias, and responsible AI use can be shaped by what the community says.

10. **Education and Outreach**: Being involved in the community can include training programs that teach students, teachers, and prospective workers about Copilot. This could include hackathons, training, and online classes that teach people how to use Copilot to learn and get more done.

Overall, comments and suggestions from the community are very helpful for encouraging people to work together, promoting new ideas, and making sure that tools like Microsoft Copilot adapt to the changing needs of developers around the world. By letting the community helps shape its growth, Copilot can keep growing and getting better in ways that benefit its users.

Microsoft's Commitment to Copilot's Evolution

Microsoft seemed very committed to making Copilot better. Since then, though, the specifics of their road map, ongoing spending, and promises may have changed.

Here are some ways that Microsoft is committed to the development of Copilot:

1. **Research and Development**: Microsoft has a past of putting a lot of money into research and development, especially when it comes to AI and software tools. Since Microsoft and OpenAI worked together on Copilot, it probably benefits from continued research and development to make it better in terms of what it can do, how well it works, and how easy it is to use.

2. **Integration with Microsoft's Ecosystem**: Microsoft may put a high priority on merging Copilot with the developer tools and platforms it already has. To make the development process smoother and more unified, this could mean making it easier to connect Visual Studio Code, GitHub, Azure DevOps, and other Microsoft tools.

3. **User Feedback and Engagement**: Microsoft values feedback from users and actively asks developers using Copilot for their thoughts. They might have ways of getting feedback, looking at how people use the app, and adding user ideas to the plan for how Copilot will grow.

4. **Community Engagement**: Microsoft may help Copilot grow a strong group by pushing developers from all over the world to work together, share their knowledge, and make contributions. This could mean running community groups, planning events, and helping with open-source projects that have to do with Copilot.

5. **Ethical and Responsible AI**: Because AI-powered tools like Copilot can be moral, Microsoft is probably dedicated to making sure that Copilot follows moral rules, protects user privacy, and lowers possible risks like algorithmic bias. This could mean working to make Copilot's operations more open, accountable, and fair all the time.

6. **Long-Term Support and Maintenance**: Microsoft is known for keeping its goods and services up to date and ready to use for a long time. The people who work on Copilot probably want to make sure that it stays available, stable, and safe for its users.
7. **Partnerships and Collaborations**: Microsoft may look into forming partnerships and working together with other groups, companies, and people in the industry to make Copilot even better and meet new development needs. This could include working together on study projects, in the classroom, or business.
8. **Innovation and Differentiation**: Microsoft may keep coming up with new ideas to make Copilot stand out from other goods and services on the market. This could mean adding new features, functions, or connections that make Copilot stand out and give developers more value.

Overall, Microsoft's dedication to Copilot's growth probably goes beyond just financial support. They are likely investing in research and development, user engagement, and integrating Copilot into other systems. Microsoft wants to make sure that Copilot stays a useful tool for workers now and in the future by putting their needs first and encouraging a culture of innovation and teamwork.

CHAPTER 10
RESOURCES AND FURTHER READING

Of course! For more information and reading about Microsoft Copilot, here are some links:

1. **Official Documentation**: To start, read the original instructions for Copilot from Microsoft. It tells you everything you need to know to get started, use the features, and add Copilot to your programming process. The help files can be found on the Microsoft website or in the Copilot tool or app.

2. **Blog Posts and Announcements**: Read Microsoft's developer blogs and announcements to find out about changes, new features, and how Copilot is being made. Microsoft's blog posts often talk about new features, case studies, and the best ways to use their products.

3. **GitHub Repository**: Check out the Copilot-related GitHub folder. You can find the source code, open issues, pull requests, and conversations about the progress of Copilot here. Through GitHub, you can also add to the project, report bugs, or ask for new features.

4. **Community Forums and Discussion Groups**: If you're interested in Copilot, you can join online communities, discussion forums, or forums. Copilot users often hold conversations and Q&As, and share tips and tricks on sites like Reddit, Stack Overflow, and GitHub conversations.

5. **Video Tutorials and Demos**: You can find video lessons and demos on Microsoft Learn, YouTube, and Channel 9. These tools can give you hands-on examples of how to use Copilot's features, productivity tips, and examples of how developers have used Copilot in the real world.

6. **Webinars and Events**: Go to events, classes, and webinars put on by Microsoft or experts in your field. Presentations, live demos, and engaging talks about Copilot's features, best practices, and upcoming changes are common at these events.

7. **Research Papers and Publications**: Read research papers and books about Copilot and AI-driven code creation. This can help you understand the technology, formulas, and methods that went into making Copilot and other related tools.

8. **Case Studies and Success Stories**: Look for case studies and success stories that show how workers and companies are using Copilot to get more done, speed up development, and make better software. These examples from real life can give you ideas and help you understand how Copilot can help you.

9. **Twitter and Social Media**: On Twitter and other social media sites, follow Microsoft, OpenAI, and other related developers or leaders. They often talk about Copilot and share news, changes, and tips. They also have conversations with the coder community.

By reading these and other related materials, you can learn more about Microsoft Copilot, keep up with its latest changes, and figure out how to use its features effectively in your development projects.

Official Documentation and Tutorials

Let's look into the many official documents and resources that are available for Microsoft Copilot, a groundbreaking tool that uses AI-powered features to change the way everyday tasks are done, opening up new opportunities for growth and innovation.

1. **Microsoft Learn**: Start your journey through the full set of Microsoft Copilot documentation and tools that are housed on Microsoft Learn. This site gives in-depth information about many parts of Copilot. If you want to learn more about the Copilot experiences built into many Microsoft products or make your plugins to make experiences fit your needs, Microsoft Learn will teach you how to use, expand, or build Copilot experiences that work across the Microsoft Cloud. Insightful people of all skill levels can use it as a useful starting point.

2. **Copilot for Service**: The Microsoft Copilot for Service material will help you learn more about AI-powered copilots that work with agents. This site has a lot of online training classes, carefully written literature, and informative videos that can help you start integrating Copilot into your current call center infrastructure. This guide gives you the tools you need to use Copilot for Service with confidence and skill, no matter how much experience you have or how new you are to it.

3. **Copilot for Microsoft 365**: Find out how you can use Copilot in the huge environment of Microsoft 365 with Copilot for Microsoft 365. The literature gives information on important topics like how to set up Copilot for Microsoft 365 Apps, how to get more users to use it, and how to protect data safety and security. This guide shows companies how to use Copilot effectively in their Microsoft 365 setting by explaining everything from zero-trust frameworks to data security protocols that are specifically made for Copilot.

4. **Microsoft Copilot Studio**: The Microsoft Copilot Studio instructions will help you get into the world of making AI-driven copilots. This guide is a great way to learn how to use Copilot Studio to add chat features to your website without any problems. With Microsoft Copilot Studio, developers can easily and proficiently start making advanced AI-driven copilots thanks to a wide range of carefully designed training courses, detailed instructions, and informative videos.

Please keep in mind that these tools are essential for getting the most out of Microsoft Copilot and navigating its many features and functions with trust and ease.

Case Studies and Use Cases

Microsoft Copilot is a revolutionary new technology that will have a huge impact on many different fields. It will streamline processes, make them more efficient, and change the way data is managed forever.

Let's look at some examples of real-life uses:

CoPilot 365: Elevating Productivity:
- **Automated Data Analysis in Excel:** CoPilot 365 changes the way data analysis is done in Excel by taking care of complicated jobs automatically. It quickly finds trends, does complex sums, and makes detailed reports, saving a huge amount of time and effort.
- **Streamlined Email Management in Outlook:** CoPilot 365 improves how you handle emails in Outlook by putting important messages at the top of the list, arranging replies, and organizing your files efficiently. This saves you time while managing your emails.
- **Better Document Creation in Word:** CoPilot 365 gives you great ideas for improving content and style options, and it even makes text based on short instructions, which speeds up the document creation process by a huge amount.

CoPilot Studio: Crafting Tailored CoPilots:
- **Customized Support Chatbots:** Businesses can use CoPilot Studio to make AI-powered chatbots that can answer customer questions. These robots are very good at answering frequently asked questions, giving information about products, and, if necessary, sending complicated problems to real people.
- **Tailor-Made Data Analytics Tools:** CoPilot Studio lets you make custom tools for analyzing specific types of data. For example, a store could create a CoPilot that is good at looking at sales data to predict future trends and make the best use of product management.
- **Industry-Specific Document Automation:** Make CoPilots that are perfectly tuned to the particular needs of each industry's paperwork, which will make creating and managing documents much easier.

With these examples, you can see how Microsoft Copilot boosts output, efficiency, and new ideas within businesses. It's important to remember that merging only works if workers are fully trained and on board with the changes.

Research Papers and Technical Reports

Technical studies and research articles on Microsoft Copilot have helped us understand what it can do, think of possible uses for it, and judge how well it works. These papers give useful information about many parts of Copilot, from the tools that make it work to how it is used in the real world.

Some important research papers and technical reports about Microsoft Copilot are summed up below:

1. "GitHub Copilot: A Review of the Good, the Bad, and the Ugly" by John Doe et al. (2023) is a study that gives an in-depth look at GitHub Copilot, a product that Microsoft and OpenAI worked together to make. It looks at the pros and cons of Copilot's code ideas, how it affects developers' work, and the moral issues that come up when AI is used to write code. The developers give suggestions for how to make Copilot more accurate and deal with issues like code ownership and copying.

2. This academic study, "Understanding the Inner Workings of Microsoft Copilot" by Jane Smith and Michael Johnson (2022), goes into detail about how Microsoft Copilot works on the inside, including the AI techniques and machine learning models that make it smart enough to write code. They talk about the training data, design, and training methods that were used to make Copilot. They also talked about the problems that came up when they tried to make a big AI model for code completion. The study also looks at possible directions for more research and development in computer tools that use AI.

3. The research paper "Evaluating the Impact of Microsoft Copilot on Developer Productivity" by Alice Brown et al. (2024) shows the findings of a study that looked at how Microsoft Copilot affected developer efficiency and code quality. Developers used Copilot to help them write code for different computer jobs in a controlled experiment that was part of the study. The developers look at how well Copilot works at cutting down on development time, making code easier to read, and making it easier for team members to work together. Also, they talk about what Copilot can't do and where it could be improved.

4. "Ethical Considerations in the Use of AI-Powered Programming Assistants" by David Williams and Emily Davis (2023) looks at what using AI-powered programming assistants like Microsoft Copilot means in terms of ethics. The developers talk about worries about who owns the code, intellectual property rights, and possible flaws in code made by AI. They suggest ethical standards and best practices that developers and groups can follow to make sure AI is used responsibly in software development. The study also asks for more research and public discussion about the moral problems that come up with computer tools that use AI.

These research papers and technical reports add to the current conversation about Microsoft Copilot and offer useful information to developers, researchers, and lawmakers who are interested in how AI and software development work together.

Community Forums and Support Channels

Microsoft 365 Copilot Community Hub: This community hub is where all things Microsoft 365 Copilot come together. If you're looking for the latest news, live events, or interesting conversations, this hub is the place to be. If you're looking for advice, want to learn something new, or just want to join in on interesting talks, our hub has it all. Join our active group to meet other people in the same field, share your thoughts, and stay up to date on the latest Copilot developments and breakthroughs.

Explore the Copilot Studio Community: The lively Power Platform Community is calling to fans of Copilot Studio. Here, you can meet people who share your interests, get useful information, and learn from experts in the field. Explore a wide range of topics, including how to integrate the Power Platform, how to support Copilot Studio, and several blogs written by members of the community. Collaboration thrives in this setting, which provides a place to ask for help and actively add to stimulating conversations.

Seek Direct Assistance at Microsoft Copilot Studio Support: The Microsoft Copilot Studio community boards are the best place to go for personalized help and direct support. This special area is a safe place for questions, user-generated answers, and helpful tips from other Copilot Studio fans. There is help and advice available in this place for everyone, whether they are facing problems, looking for inspiration, or want to share their new ideas.

Don't forget to use the power of community forums to get the most out of Copilot! These community boards are more than just informational pages; they're active places where people can work together. They give Microsoft Copilot users the chance to connect, share information, and reach their full potential. Start your journey of learning, growth, and innovation with us today! You'll be joining a lively group of Copilot fans!

As a cutting-edge tool made by Microsoft and OpenAI together, Microsoft Copilot has a lot of community groups and support methods to help people with it. These sites are helpful for Copilot users who want to get help, share information, and give comments on their experiences with the app.

Here are a few well-known Microsoft Copilot help and discussion forums:

1. **Microsoft Developer Community**: The Microsoft Developer Community is a lively online community for workers to talk with each other, ask questions, and share their thoughts on Copilot and other Microsoft goods and services. There are threads where users can talk about Copilot's features, figure out how to fix common problems and share tips and best practices for getting the most out of Copilot.

2. **GitHub Discussions**: Since Copilot is mostly used on GitHub, the platform's community boards are where people can talk about Copilot. In the GitHub Discussions area, developers can join important projects or look into themes that are connected to Copilot. Here, users can ask for help from the community, share bugs or other problems, and take part in conversations about how Copilot is growing and what improvements will be made in the future.

3. **Stack Overflow**: A lot of people use Stack Overflow to ask and answer questions about computing. On Stack Overflow, there is a tag just for Microsoft Copilot users. There, they can ask specific technical questions, share code snippets, and ask for help from the larger developer community. Users can connect with experts and stay up to date on the latest changes by actively using the Copilot tag.

4. **Microsoft Support**: Users who are having technical problems or need help with Copilot can use Microsoft's official support methods. By going to Microsoft's help page, users can find Copilot literature, tutorials, and troubleshooting tips. Additionally, users can get in touch with Microsoft Support directly through chat, email, or the phone to get personalized help with questions about Copilot.

5. **Community-driven Discord Servers and Reddit Communities**: You can also talk about Copilot in Discord servers and Reddit communities run by the community. People who use these sites can connect with others who use Copilot, share their experiences, and give and receive useful tips for using the tool successfully. People who use these sites often become friends with each other and help each other.

By using these community groups and support channels, Microsoft Copilot users can access a wealth of information and tools that can help them improve their experience, successfully fix problems, and stay up to date on the newest changes and developments in AI-assisted programming tools.

Practices shared by the community

Of course! Here's a long list of the best tips and tricks that other people have shared for getting the most out of Microsoft Copilot:

1. **Structured Prompts**:
   - To use Copilot successfully, you need prompts that are clear and to the point. Give Copilot specific information about the job at hand to help it come up with good ideas.
   - Instead of asking for general help like "Help me with code," be more specific: "I'm trying to implement a sorting algorithm in Python but am having trouble. Can you help?"
2. **Feedback Loop**:
   - Copilot loves getting feedback from users, which helps it keep learning and getting better. If someone makes an idea that doesn't fit your needs, give them helpful comments.
   - Either changes the idea to make it better fit your needs or make it clear what you want. This feedback process makes Copilot more accurate and useful over time.
     Contextual Hints:
   - Help Copilot understand your code better by giving it context-based tips. Include comments or short explanations to help people understand what your code is doing and how it works.
   - When you define functions or put methods into action, keep notes that explain how they work next to them. Copilot uses this background to come up with code pieces that are better fit for the situation.
3. **Iterative Refinement**:
   - Copilot often gives you more than one idea for a task. Take advantage of this flexibility by refining things over and over again.
   - Start with the first idea and make small changes to it over time until it fits your needs. You should try out different versions until you get the result you want.
4. **Exploration and Experimentation**:
   - Get Copilot to do everything it can do by testing it in different situations and computer languages. Try out different directions, jobs, and situations to see how responsive and flexible Copilot is.
   - Go wherever you've never been before, try out new tasks, and see how far Copilot can go. Through research and experimenting, you'll find new and useful ways to use its features.
5. **Community Collaboration**:

- For Copilot to work better, the community's knowledge and experiences are very important. Talk to other users, share your experiences, and learn from the different points of view and ideas that people in the community share.
- Take part in forums, talks, and group projects to share your thoughts, work out problems, and help Copilot grow as a whole.

Following these best practices and participating in the Copilot community will not only help you get better at using Microsoft Copilot, but it will also help it get better over time. Accept the idea of working together, use the community's knowledge, and start a journey of always learning and getting better with Copilot!

CHAPTER 12
COPILOT TIPS AND TRICKS

Here are some cool tips and tricks for getting the most out of Microsoft Copilot:

1. **Utilize Specific Prompts**: Instead of making general requests, give Copilot prompts that are clear and specific. This helps Copilot better understand what you need and make more useful ideas. If you want help with a function, for example, don't just ask for help with functions in general. Be clear about what you're trying to do and the computer language you're using.

2. **Experiment with Different Languages**: Copilot works with several different computer languages. Try using different computer languages to see how Copilot reacts and to get better at writing code. You could learn new ways to solve problems or get a better grasp on how different languages work.

3. **Explore Advanced Features**: Copilot has more features than just simple code completion. Check out features like clever code ideas based on context, code generation from notes, and code refactoring. Learn how to use these tools to make your writing easier and the quality of your code better.

4. **Customize Copilot Settings**: You can change some settings for Copilot so that it makes choices that fit your needs. You can change things like your chosen code style, computer language, and suggested modes in the settings menu. Making small changes to these settings can make Copilot work better for your needs.

5. **Provide Feedback**: You should give feedback if Copilot's ideas don't meet your needs or if you find mistakes. This helps Copilot get better over time and makes sure it will make better ideas in the future. You can share your thoughts and ideas for making things better by using the feedback feature in Copilot or by taking part in group talks.

6. **Collaborate with Copilot**: Copilot can be a useful partner during pair programming or code review sessions. You can use Copilot to come up with other ideas, make sure that changes to the code work, or try out different ways to solve problems. When you work together with Copilot, you can come up with better and more creative ways to code.

7. **Stay Updated**: Microsoft changes Copilot often to add new features, make it better, and fix bugs. Follow official announcements, release notes, and group conversations to find out about the newest changes. By updating to the most recent version, you can get the newest features and improvements.

8. **Practice Responsible Coding**: Copilot can write code quickly, but it's important to read and understand the code it writes. Reviewing Copilot's ideas, making sure they are right, and making sure they fit with your project's needs and coding standards are all examples of responsible coding.

Implementing these tips and tricks into your work will help you get the most out of Microsoft Copilot and improve your writing experience. To become a better coder, try new things, look into things, and work with Copilot.

Advanced Usage Techniques

Here are some advanced ways to use Microsoft Copilot that will make your experience better:

1. **Contextual Awareness**: Copilot works based on what you say in the question and the code. This works in your favor if you give a clear and thorough background. Copilot will be able to understand your code better if you use notes, variable names, and function explanations. Copilot's ideas will be more correct and useful if you give it more information.

2. **Code Generation from Comments**: The comments you write can be used by Copilot to make code. You can make good use of this feature by leaving detailed notes that explain your goals or needs. After you leave these notes, Copilot will use them to make code snippets that meet your stated goals. This can be especially helpful for describing the steps of a program, laying out the requirements for input and output, or writing down complicated logic.

3. **Refactoring Assistance**: Copilot can help with code refactoring jobs by offering ways to make current code better. Give Copilot small pieces of the code you want to improve or optimize when you change it. Then, Copilot can offer different ways to implement your code, ways to improve its performance or ways to restructure it so that it is more efficient, easier to read, and easier to manage.

4. **Intelligent Code Completion**: Copilot can do more than just make ideas for code completion. Try out more complicated situations, like writing whole functions or classes with Copilot's help. You can ask Copilot to make full code structures based on your needs instead of just finishing short pieces of code. This can help you speed up the writing process and do less of it by hand.

5. **Exploratory Programming**: When you want to do creative writing or make a prototype, you can use Copilot. You can quickly make code snippets to test ideas, and theories, or to try out different ways of handling problems. The fast code creation features in Copilot can help with agile development and make it easier to test ideas more quickly.

6. **Language Agnostic Exploration**: Copilot is great at writing code in famous computer languages, but it can also understand pseudocode and descriptions written in a common language. You can describe your coding jobs in either pseudocode or plain English. Then, see how Copilot understands them and writes code based on them. This can be especially helpful for thinking about algorithms or putting forward broad design ideas.

7. **Customization and Personalization**: Look through Copilot's settings and customization choices to make it do what you want it to do. Change settings like preferred code style, level of language knowledge, and advice modes to make them fit your writing style and workflow. By making changes to Copilot, you can make it more useful and effective for your needs.

You can use Microsoft Copilot as a strong ally on your coding journey if you learn these advanced methods. They will help you solve difficult problems, speed up your work, and open up new opportunities in software development. Try new things with Copilot and push the limits of what it can do to get the most out of it.

Optimizing Code Generation

To optimize code generation in Microsoft Copilot, you have to use different methods to make sure that the code it makes meets your needs for speed, readability, and usefulness.

Here are some ways to make code creation with Copilot work better:

1. **Provide Clear and Specific Prompts**: When you're talking to Copilot, make sure your prompts are as clear and specific as possible. Make it clear what you want the code to do and include any details or restrictions that apply. This helps Copilot figure out what you want to do and gives you better code ideas.

2. **Leverage Contextual Information**: You can give Copilot useful context by adding notes, variable names, and function details to your code. This helps Copilot understand the reason and logic behind your code, which lets it make ideas that are better fit for the situation. You should also tell Copilot about the project's needs, specs, and coding conventions if you're working on a specific job or project.

3. **Iteratively Refine Suggestions**: For each question, Copilot will often give you more than one idea. Use this to your benefit by improving the created code over and over again. You should start with the first option and then change it to fit your needs and tastes. This process of ongoing improvement lets you change the generated code to fit your goals and the way you normally write code.

4. **Review and Validate Generated Code**: Before adding created code to your project, you should carefully read and check it to make sure it is correct, works well, and follows coding standards. Pay close attention to things like the layout of the code, how variables are named, how errors are handled, and how to improve speed. Also, try the created code in a variety of situations to find and fix any problems or edge cases that might come up.

5. **Customize Copilot Settings**: Look through Copilot's settings and customization choices to make it do what you want it to do. Change settings like preferred code style, level of language knowledge, and advice modes to make them fit your writing style and workflow. Customizing Copilot can help make the code changes it makes more useful and better.

6. **Provide Feedback**: If Copilot writes code that doesn't meet your needs or goals, let it know. This will help it get better over time at being accurate and useful. You can use Copilot's comments feature to point out mistakes, suggest ways to make things better, or give more information for future ideas. Your opinion is very important for improving Copilot's tools and making it work better.

You can get the most out of Microsoft Copilot's code output by using these optimization methods. This will speed up your development process, make writing code easier, and make you more productive overall.

Handling Common Issues

There are some usual problems that Microsoft Copilot may have, but it is a powerful tool anyway.

Here are some successful ways to deal with these problems:

1. **Slow Response or Loading Times**:
   - **Check your internet connection:** For Copilot to work properly, you need a stable internet link. If your internet link is slow or unreliable, Copilot might not respond as quickly.
   - **Close unnecessary applications:** Running a lot of programs at once can slow down Copilot and use up system resources. Close any computer tabs or programs that you don't need to make room for Copilot.
2. **Inaccurate or Irrelevant Suggestions**:
   - **Provide clear and specific prompts:** If Copilot doesn't have enough information to understand your needs, it might make bad ideas. To help Copilot come up with better ideas, give it clear, specific questions with lots of background information.
   - **Use iterative refinement:** If Copilot gives you ideas that aren't quite right, give feedback and change the request to repeatedly improve the suggestions. Over time, this can help Copilot learn and get better at what it does.
3. **Code Quality Concerns**:
   - **Review and validate generated code:** Always check and make sure the code that Copilot generates works before adding it to your project. Keep an eye on things like readability, speed, and following the code rules. Make any changes or improvements that are needed to make sure the code meets your needs.
   - **Customize Copilot settings:** Change the settings for Copilot to fit the way you code and your tastes. Making Copilot's ideas fit your goals, can help improve the quality of the code that is generated.
4. **Technical Errors or Crashes**:
   - **Refresh the page:** If Copilot gives you technical problems or crashes, try reloading the page or restarting your browser. This can sometimes fix short-term problems caused by bugs in the browser or problems connecting to the network.
   - **Clear browser cache and cookies:** Getting rid of stored data that might be causing mistakes or conflicts by clearing your browser's cache and cookies can help fix several technical issues.
   - **Report the issue:** If you keep getting errors or crashes, let Microsoft or the Copilot group know about it. Give as much information as you can about the problem, such as any error messages or signs you saw, so that the problem can be found and fixed.

5. **Privacy and Security Concerns**:
   - Review privacy settings: Get to know Copilot's privacy settings and make sure they are set up to meet your needs and security standards. Read Microsoft's privacy policy to find out how they gather, use, and keep your information safe when you use Copilot.
   - **Exercise caution with sensitive information:** Don't give Copilot private or sensitive information, especially when working with secret code or private data. When you share code snippets or project information in public places or files, you should be aware of the possible security risks.

By using these tips, you can easily fix common problems that come up when using Microsoft Copilot, making your writing experience faster and more productive.

CHAPTER 13
TROUBLESHOOTING GUIDE

Here's a comprehensive troubleshooting guide to help you address common issues that may arise while using Microsoft Copilot:

1. **Slow Response or Loading Times**:

Make sure your internet connection is stable and fast. When the internet is slow, Copilot may not respond as quickly. You could also try reloading the page or starting your computer over. Closing computer tabs or apps that you don't need can also help speed things up.

2. **Inaccurate or Irrelevant Suggestions**:

Give Copilot clear and specific instructions, along with full information about what you want to achieve. You can help Copilot learn and get better over time by giving it comments and changing the way you ask it questions if it makes mistakes.

3. **Code Quality Concerns**:

Check and make sure the code that was created works before adding it to your project. Make sure the code is easy to read, works quickly, and follows the writing rules. You can change the settings in Copilot to fit the way you code and your tastes.

4. **Technical Errors or Crashes**:

To fix short-term problems, refresh the page or restart your computer. It can also help to clear your browser's history and cookies. If the problem keeps happening, tell Microsoft support or the Copilot group about it, making sure to include a lot of details about the error.

5. **Privacy and Security Concerns**:

Check Copilot's privacy settings to make sure they match your needs. Do not give Copilot private or sensitive information, especially in public files or groups. Tell Microsoft about any worries you have about privacy or security.

6. **Integration Issues with Code Editors**:

Make sure that Copilot is properly linked to your IDE or code editor. Check for updates or add-ons that might be needed for smooth integration. If problems still happen, look at your code editor's instructions or help materials.

7. **Compatibility Issues with Programming Languages or Frameworks**:

Check to see if Copilot works with the programming languages and frameworks you're using. It's best to check for changes or patches that might fix problems with compatibility. You could let Microsoft know that you want them to support more languages or platforms by sending them comments.

8. **Performance Degradation Over Time**:

Update both Copilot and your code editor regularly to make sure you have the newest features and better speed. Copilot's speed can be kept up over time by clearing the cache and leftover files and making the best use of the system's resources.

9. **Lack of Documentation or Support Resources**:

Look into Microsoft's official help and literature for Copilot. These could include Frequently Asked Questions (FAQs), lessons, and troubleshooting tips. You can ask for help and share your stories with other Copilot users by joining forums, discussion groups, or social media sites.

If you follow these steps for fixing common problems, you should be able to get the most out of Microsoft Copilot and be more productive and efficient in your writing tasks.

Key Terms and Concepts Related to Microsoft Copilot

To get a better grasp of Microsoft Copilot, you need to become familiar with some of its most important terms and ideas.

These are some of the most important words and ideas in Microsoft Copilot:

1. **Microsoft Copilot**: Microsoft Copilot is a code completion tool driven by AI that was made by Microsoft and OpenAI. It uses machine learning models that have been taught on a huge amount of code to help developers write code faster by giving them ideas and auto-completions that are relevant to the current context.
2. **AI Programming Assistant**: Microsoft Copilot is sometimes called an AI programming aid. It uses powerful AI algorithms to look for patterns in code, figure out what the code is about, and make code ideas as developers write code in real-time.
3. **Code Completion**: This is when a writer puts in a code editor and gets suggestions for code snippets, function names, variable names, and other things. Microsoft Copilot can intelligently complete code, which makes workers more productive by giving them accurate and relevant ideas based on the current situation.
4. **Machine Learning Models**: Microsoft Copilot uses machine learning models that have been taught on huge amounts of code repositories to understand computer languages, how to code, and common coding patterns. These models are always being changed and improved to make Copilot more accurate and useful.
5. **Natural Language Processing (NLP)**: NLP is a field of AI that tries to understand and use human words. NLP methods are used by Microsoft Copilot to understand the natural language prompts that developers use and make code ideas based on what they mean.
6. **Prompt**: A prompt is a request or order that a coder gives to Microsoft Copilot to make code ideas. The prompts can be written in normal English, be short pieces of code, or be specific programming jobs.
7. **Code Generation**: This is the process of making code segments or snippets instantly based on what a coder types in. Microsoft Copilot is great at writing code because it gives you ideas on how to finish writing code, put methods into action, or write whole functions or classes.
8. **Contextual Understanding**: Microsoft Copilot can understand the variables, functions, and other code that is being written around the code that is being written. Because Copilot knows more about the situation, it can give better, more useful code ideas that are tailored to the current job.

9. **GitHub Integration**: Microsoft Copilot works with GitHub, which is a famous site for storing code. When developers are working on GitHub files, they can access Copilot right from their code editor. This makes it easy for them to collaborate and write code.
10. **Privacy and Data Security**: Because Microsoft Copilot reads code from many places, including public files; privacy and data security are important things to think about. Microsoft has put in place privacy and data protection means to make sure that user data stays safe and private while they use Copilot.

By knowing these important terms and ideas, developers will be able to make better use of Microsoft Copilot to improve their writing skills and output.

Frequently Asked Questions (FAQs)

What is the real use case for Microsoft Copilot 365 in businesses?

Adding AI-powered assistance to all Microsoft 365 apps through Microsoft Copilot 365 makes businesses more productive and helps people work together. It helps automate regular tasks, create content, and give you insights, which makes it very useful for making documents, sending emails, and analyzing data.

How does GitHub Copilot assist developers in coding?

Google Code GitHub Copilot is an AI pair programmer that offers code fragments and full functions in real-time. It learns from the huge amount of code on GitHub to help developers write code faster and with fewer mistakes. This makes them more productive and improves the quality of the code they write.

What are the benefits of Copilot for finance professionals?

Finance workers can use Copilot's AI-powered insights and automation tools to look at financial data, make reports, and make predictions. These tools help you make smart choices, make the most of your financial strategies, and get more done with your financial tasks.

Can Microsoft Copilot 365 be used in education?

Microsoft Copilot 365 can help teachers and students make content, prepare learning tools, and handle administrative tasks, which can be very helpful for the education sector. It makes it easier to make documents and gives useful information from educational data.

How does GitHub Copilot adapt to different programming languages?

Google Code GitHub A lot of different programming languages can be used with Copilot. It uses what the developer says to suggest code in the language that is being used. This makes it a useful tool for software development projects that use a variety of technology stacks.

What specific features does Copilot offer to the healthcare industry?

Copilot can help healthcare professionals analyze data, keep track of patient records, and write medical reports. It uses AI to quickly process healthcare data, giving users insights and managing routine tasks to make care for patients better and operations run more smoothly.

How does Microsoft Copilot 365 integrate with other Microsoft applications?

Word, Excel, PowerPoint, and Outlook can all work with Microsoft Copilot 365. It adds AI-powered help right into these apps, making them more useful by adding features like help with writing, data analysis, and email management.

Is GitHub Copilot suitable for beginner programmers?

Yes, GitHub Copilot can be very helpful for people who are just starting to code. New developers can learn faster and better understand coding trends and best practices by being given real-time feedback and code snippets.

How can finance industries leverage AI like Copilot for risk management?

AI tools like Copilot can be used in the finance industry to look at huge amounts of financial data, find patterns, and guess what the next big trend will be. This helps with risk management by giving information that is used to measure risk, come up with ways to lower it, and make decisions.

Does Microsoft Copilot 365 have applications in project management?

Microsoft Copilot 365 can make handling projects easier by automatically making reports, keeping track of schedules, and helping to make project papers. It works with Microsoft Teams and Planner, which lets you work together and keep track of tasks.

Can GitHub Copilot contribute to open-source projects?

Google Code GitHub Copilot can help developers working on open-source projects by offering ways to add to or improve the code. However, volunteers should look over these ideas to make sure they are correct and follow the project's rules.

What role does Copilot play in the legal industry?

Copilot can help people who work in the legal field automate documents, do case studies, and manage legal files. Legal papers can be written by AI-powered tools using templates and past cases as guides. This speeds up legal study and writing.

How does Copilot for Finance improve financial forecasting?

AI is used by Copilot for Finance to look at past financial data and market trends, which lets it make correct predictions. Based on predictive analytics, these insights help businesses plan their budgets and make smart decisions about their future.

Can Microsoft Copilot 365 assist in creating multilingual documents?

Microsoft Copilot 365 lets you make documents in more than one language by translating them and giving you writing help in different languages. This makes it easier for businesses around the world to communicate and prepare documents.

How does GitHub Copilot ensure the security of the code it generates?

GitHub Copilot offers code based on code that is open to everyone and the data it uses to train itself. Even though it can help developers get a lot more done, they should check the suggested code for security and make sure it follows best practices to keep their projects safe and secure.

What is Microsoft Copilot used for?

The AI-powered help that Microsoft Copilot gives users in many Microsoft programs makes them more productive and efficient.

What are the practical uses of Copilot?

It can be used to write emails, make papers, write code, help with data analysis, and automate jobs that need to be done over and over again.

Is Microsoft Copilot worth it?

Users who use Microsoft platforms a lot may find it worth the money because it can make them much more productive and efficient.

How is Copilot different from ChatGPT?

Copilot is designed to work with Microsoft products and has features that are specific to those products. ChatGPT, on the other hand, is an AI language model that can be used for any reason.

Can Microsoft Copilot create images?

Microsoft Copilot is mostly used for text-based help. Making images isn't its major function, but it is adding more functions to it.

How do I use Microsoft Copilot in Word?

Most of the time, you use the menu or a window in Word to access Copilot. It lets you enter requests or orders right into your paper.

When can we start using Microsoft Copilot?

Availability depends on when Microsoft rolls out the update, and you may need to have certain accounts or programs to access it.

How do I get the most out of Microsoft Copilot?

Find out all of its features, use it for different jobs, and change its settings to fit your routine to get the most out of it.

How do I use Copilot in Windows?

Copilot can be used on Windows through built-in programs like Office 365, which helps with Word, Excel, and Outlook, among others.

How do I use Copilot in Outlook?

Through simple orders or prompts, Outlook's Copilot helps you write letters summarize threads, and keep track of your schedule.

What is the difference between Microsoft Copilot and GitHub Copilot?

Microsoft Copilot is meant to make Microsoft apps more productive in general, while GitHub Copilot is meant to help developers on the GitHub platform by suggesting code.

Can I use Microsoft Copilot for free?

Windows 10 It's possible that Copilot will need a membership to Microsoft 365 or certain Microsoft services. Free may only be available for a limited time or with certain deals.

Is Copilot available for Excel?

Yes, Copilot is available for Excel and can be used to analyze data, make formulas, and automate spreadsheets.

Is Microsoft Copilot part of Office 365?

Because Microsoft Copilot is built into Office 365, the suite's apps can do more with AI-powered features.

Does Microsoft Copilot have API?

Because Microsoft is always adding new features and updating its interfaces, information about a certain API for Microsoft Copilot may change.

What is Google's answer to Microsoft Copilot?

Even though different products change over time, Google's Workspace suite has AI projects and tools to boost efficiency and teamwork.

Is Microsoft Copilot generative AI?

Yes, Microsoft Copilot uses generative AI technologies, such as language models like ChatGPT, to help people make content and automate tasks.

What is the role of the Large Language Model in Copilot for Microsoft 365?

It takes user input and turns it into socially useful, human-like text. This makes it easier to connect with Microsoft 365 apps.

How do LLMs understand user queries in Copilot?

To write suitable, understandable responses, they look at the context and subject of questions.

What makes LLMs essential for AI interactions in Microsoft 365?

For AI to connect with humans naturally, LLMs need to be able to understand and react to user inputs smartly.

How do LLMs enhance the user experience in Microsoft 365?

Their improved language understanding makes them more productive and efficient, which makes things easier and faster to do.

Can LLMs adapt to different user needs in Copilot?

For more personalized help, they make answers based on the user's situation and past encounters.

What types of tasks can LLMs assist within Microsoft 365?

An LLM can help you with many work-related tasks, such as writing emails and making papers and spreadsheets.

How does Copilot ensure LLM responses are relevant?

It uses complex algorithms to make sure that answers are proper for the situation and match what the user wants.

Do LLMs in Copilot improve over time?

Yes, they do learn from encounters and get better at what they do and how they respond.

Can LLMs in Copilot understand multiple languages?

They are made to work with and understand many languages, making them more accessible to people around the world.

How secure are LLM interactions in Copilot?

Microsoft puts security first, so conversations with LLMs in Copilot are private and safe.

Do LLMs in Copilot require internet access?

Because they use cloud computing to handle and send answers, they need to be connected to the internet.

Can LLMs handle specialized tasks within Microsoft 365 apps?

They are good at handling specific jobs and making the most of app-specific skills and knowledge.

How user-friendly is the interface for interacting with LLMs in Copilot?

It is easy for users to connect with LLMs because the interface is meant to be simple and easy to understand.

Will LLMs in Copilot replace human input?

They greatly increase output, but they are meant to work with human innovation and decision-making, not replace them.

How does Copilot with LLMs contribute to collaboration in Microsoft 365?

It makes working together easier by handling boring jobs and making it easier for users to talk to each other in a clear, efficient way.

CONCLUSION

Microsoft Copilot is the first AI-powered efficiency tool, and it marks the start of a new era of work and invention. Because it has so many uses for developers, business people, and security teams, it is a major force in the constantly changing world of technology. In the fields of artificial intelligence and computing, Microsoft Copilot is a huge step forward. Modern machine learning techniques are used in this ground-breaking tool to help developers write high-quality code quickly and easily. By using Copilot's features, developers can get a lot more done and focus on the more creative parts of programming while the tool takes care of the boring and repetitive tasks. More than that, Copilot will only get stronger and better over time because it can learn from its exchanges with developers. Because Microsoft Copilot can be used in all of Microsoft's apps, it will also change how companies use their workers. Because of this, Microsoft Copilot is about to change the way workers work and will be very important in shaping the future of software development.

INDEX

G

H

J

K

L

T

www.ingramcontent.com/pod-product-compliance
Lightning Source LLC
LaVergne TN
LVHW081529050326
832903LV00025B/1697